To Mike
with ♡

W9-AAY-971

Praise for *Heart and Sell*

"*Heart and Sell* bridges the gap between the new science of selling and the realities of today's highly informed and equally overwhelmed customer who demands and deserves a more personal sales approach. Levitin's expertise is readily apparent in this read and expertly blends neuroscience, heart and humor to create a powerful resource for anyone who wishes for success in sales."

—Michael Brown, CEO, Hilton Grand Vacations

"If you practice just one of Levitin's 'universal truths', you'll have immediate success. So, why not put all ten into action…and watch out! A tour de force for anyone interested in selling, serving or living a more authentic life."

—Shep Hyken, *New York Times* best-selling author of
The Amazement Revolution

"Shari is an amazing speaker and author. *Heart and Sell* is filled with wit, wisdom and humor. A MUST for anyone selling anything."

—Patricia Fripp, past president of National Speakers Association, CSP,
CPAE sales presentation trainer, keynote speaker, executive speech coach

"It's been said that nothing happens in this world until a sale is made. It's also been said that there's nothing more important in life than relationships. Shari blends these two concepts beautifully. Going beyond the 'how-to,' this book gets to the 'why' that only the top salespeople understand."

—Dan Baker PhD, Dan Baker Consulting, author of
What Happy People Know, lecturer, executive coach, and consultant

"Shari Levitin talks about eliminating excuses and taking responsibility in this book. So no excuses—buy this book and take responsibility for your sales success. *Heart and Sell* is a winner."

—Colleen Stanley, president of Sales Leadership,
author of *Emotional Intelligence for Sales Success*

"Full of Levitin's usual wit, compassion and humor. Her fans will be delighted and sales leaders can gain new actionable and useable tools to increase profits and create more satisfied customers. It's refreshing to see science-backed research combined with heart and authenticity. Timely and necessary!"

—Fiona Downing, senior vice president,
Development & Operations, RCI

"Heart and Sell is an essential must-read—but don't for a moment think this is a book only for sales professionals. Anyone in the business of persuading others will walk away richer for having read it."

—Maria Margenot, senior vice president, sales development,
recruiting & training, Wyndham Vacation Ownership

"Establishing trust through relationship building is critical, yet it's something sales professionals sometimes forget. Shari highlights the importance of establishing, maintaining, and growing trust between buyers and sellers through reliability, honesty, and integrity. Shari drives home her wisdom with passion and emotion, helping readers remember her message through storytelling, anecdotes, and vignettes. Shari's wisdom is transformative. I can't recommend *Heart and Sell* strongly enough."

—Ken Allred, founder and CEO of Primary Intelligence

"Heart and Sell is brilliant. Shari's approach is fresh, funny and practical. It's loaded with useable ideas and will quickly become the new method of selling for the entire resort industry."

—Eric White, director of Pacific Sun Marketing

"Heart and Sell is incredibly powerful and insightful. Every sales professional should have these skills in their tool chest. This book will not only help you close more deals but will renew your spirit and your life purpose."

—Lt. Col. Rob "Waldo" Waldman, MBA, CSP, CPAE, Your
Wingman, Member of the Speaker Hall of Fame,
New York Times best-selling author of *Never Fly Solo*

"This is a fantastic read and a breath of fresh air from the 'pitch' style sales training. It is the connection of heart, caring and incorporating that into the process which creates happy new clients for years to come...this is the next level of training we are striving for here and is 100 percent effective."
—Doug Saunders, project director, Vida Vacations, Mexico

"Shari is a star! I rarely make it all the way through business books. But hers, I read cover to cover!"
—Kathryn (Katie) Hoffman Abby, Assistant Dean, Corporate Outreach, David Eccles School of Business at the University of Utah

"When it comes to selling the heart always comes before the head. In this day and age developing trust as an emotional sales bond is a critical success factor. In this book Shari teaches us how to do just that. Bravo!"
—Trish Bertuzzi, author of *The Sales Development Playbook*

Heart

AND

Sell

10 UNIVERSAL TRUTHS EVERY SALESPERSON NEEDS TO KNOW

Shari Levitin

CAREER PRESS

Wayne, NJ

HEART AND SELL
EDITED BY ROGER SHEETY
TYPESET BY PERFECTYPE, NASHVILLE, TENNESSEE
Printed in the U.S.A.

To order this title, please call toll-free 1-800-CAREER-1 (NJ and Canada: 201-848-0310) to order using VISA or MasterCard, or for further information on books from Career Press.

CAREER
PRESS

The Career Press, Inc.
12 Parish Drive
Wayne, NJ 07470
www.careerpress.com

Library of Congress Cataloging-in-Publication Data

CIP Data Available Upon Request.

DEDICATION

To my mother who I respect love and admire with all of my heart. There are no words to describe her joy, drive and compassion. But if I did have words, she'd encourage me to re-write them, to edit them just one more time, and make them better.

ACKNOWLEDGMENTS

They say writing a book is like giving birth. Having missed that experience, I can say that writing *Heart and Sell* has been the most wonderful, painful, frustrating, agonizing, joyful, and rewarding experience of my life. Similarly, the creation of this book is not something I could have done alone.

I want to start and thank my beautiful, loving family. My life shifted from black and white to color when my husband, Lee, and his son (now my adopted son), Tyler, entered my life. Thank you both for your love and understanding during the past year of 16-hour days, for always being available for discussions and editing, and for continually cheering me on.

Thank you to my father, who has always told me I could do anything I put my mind to, and to my very successful brother, Daniel, who is a role model of humility.

I am indebted to my friend and mentor, Jill Konrath. Thank you for kicking my butt and making me write a real book, rather than "a give away at the end of a poorly attended conference." Your expert guidance and generosity of spirit provides new meaning to the phrase, "There's enough to go around."

Thank you to Stanford lecturers and confidants, Lee Eisler and Marisa Handler, for helping me find my authentic voice and to learn to speak from my heart.

I am also grateful to the many friends and colleagues in the trenches in sales, mentoring, and leadership, who graciously read early chapters. They offered wisdom and advice to ensure that *Heart and Sell* is relevant to today's ever-changing consumer and the needs of the modern sales professional.

Specifically:

Katie Hoffman-Abby

Ken Allred

Dr. Dan Baker

Trish Bertuzzi

Julie Benson

Terri Cotter

Lee Eisler

Patricia Fripp

Carolyn Galvin

Erika Garcia

Michael Gehrig

Melissa Gordon

Daniel Greene

Sean Harrison

Ron Hensel

Jim Madrid

Maria Margenot

Alyson Robbins

Katie Roberts

Adam Robertson

Doug Saunders

Glenn Seninger

Will Spendlove

Colleen Stanley

Waldo Waldman

Jack Waller

Andrea Waltz

I feel an enormous amount of gratitude to those employees, strategic partners, and major clients, past and present, who were most instrumental in the success of Levitin Group during the last 20 years. Especially Kent Kozimor for his loyalty and flexibility, Terry Ferara for being my moral compass and partner, Dave Stroeve, Eric White, Geoff Balotti, Kari Bodily, Jenny Ochtera Davlin, Fiona Downing, Howard Nussbaum, Linda Clemons, Joe McGriff, Bruce Polansky, Ken May, Franz Hanning, Gordon Gurnik, Valerie Ickes, and Angela Andrews.

To my best friends, Colleen Sugerman and Susan Fredston-Hermann for your emotional support.

I could certainly not have done it if it wasn't for the tireless work of my editors: Michael Levin, who helped me uncover the heart of my message and who brought wit and humor. To Sarah Rainone for her tireless commitment to help craft the right structure and message. Also, thank you to Kelsey Fredston-Hermann for her intelligence and inquisitiveness.

Much gratitude to Lori Richardson, and the amazing women in SalesPros. Thank you for accepting me into this high-power group of women who support each other in their work, and whose mission it is to create an even better future for women sales professionals.

Finally, I would like to acknowledge the thousands of hard-working sales professionals and sales leaders who find value in our training. You put your all into every client interaction, and you do make a difference. You take rejection, pull yourself up, and give everyone your heart and soul. Above all, thanks to you.

CONTENTS

Introduction. 13

Chapter 1: Success Starts With the Growth Equation 29

Chapter 2: Emotions Drive Decision-Making 49

Chapter 3: Freedom Lives in Structure. 65

Chapter 4: In Sales, No Never Means No 87

Chapter 5: Trust Begins With Empathy. 105

Chapter 6: Integrity Matters 125

Chapter 7: Anything That Can Be Told Can Be Asked 143

Chapter 8: Emotional Commitment Precedes Economic Commitment. 163

Chapter 9: Removing Resistance Takes Persistance 183

Chapter 10: Looking for Wrongs Never Makes You Right. 207

Notes. 227

Index 233

INTRODUCTION

Balancing Heart and Sales

I don't remember the exact date it happened, but I'll never forget the feeling.

Five hours into teaching a sales seminar for a client in Mexico, I was convinced I had everyone hooked. I'd spent 15 years as a salesperson developing a system, and though I was new to the training business, my audience had taken to it pretty well. They laughed at my stories. They nodded along with my ideas. I was feeling good.

I'd just finished talking about the importance of what I call "Third-Level questions"—questions that lead you to the deeper, emotional "why" behind people's purchasing decisions—when a salesperson at the back of the room raised his hand.

"I like all of this stuff you're teaching," he said, "but won't the customer feel sort of, well, *manipulated* by all of these sales techniques?"

The room fell silent.

I had never been asked that question before

and it threw me. My whole mission was to teach ethical behaviors to salespeople. That was the point of my system: building an authentic connection.

I did my best to look confident, however I was anything but. Was this my inexperience teaching me something new, or—and this was the scarier option—*was I teaching techniques that were shallow and even manipulative?* That wasn't who I was or what I wanted to be.

I stalled for time.

"Let me think about that tonight," I said. "And we'll discuss it in the morning."

Fortunately, that evening I was invited to dinner with the top salespeople at the seminar. An older gentleman introduced himself as Apapacho.

"Apapacho?" I asked. I hadn't heard that name before.

"It's a nickname," he explained. "It means 'hugger,' or 'affectionate one.'"

Apapacho told me a little bit about his background; he'd been with the company for 25 years, was one of its top salespeople, and yet . . .

"I have a confession to make," he said. "I've never received formal sales training. I simply love my customers. I am a student of people." Apapacho had met many of his first customers when their kids were in elementary school. Now, those same children were graduating from college and raising kids of their own. He had been a fixture in their lives, sending holiday cards just after Thanksgiving with pictures of his three dogs.

"To them, I guess I'm just Apapacho!" he said.

At that moment, I knew I had my answer for the man in the back of the room, and so, the next morning, I jumped right into it.

"I want to talk to you about yesterday's question," I said. "I think you're right. If you simply use sales techniques and don't genuinely *care for* and *connect with* your customers, you'll falter. You'll sound staged, even manipulative. In fact, if that's the only way you know how to sell, you should find another profession."

The man who'd asked the question nodded. It was hitting home.

"But be careful about going too far in the other direction. If all you have is *apapacho*—that affection for your customers—and you never use any solid techniques, you'll probably do well in sales, but not as well as you could," I continued, before sharing my big realization from the night before.

"When you combine proven techniques with *apapacho*," I said. "That's when you will find true success."

At its core, this is a book about human connection. It's about how to come from a place of *apapacho* with your customers—and with everyone you meet. It's about how to use proven sales skills without losing your authenticity.

Plenty of books will help you maximize your profits and get the most out of your employees. Those books are rife with techniques to ignite and incentivize your sales force, and they have their place in the world.

This *is not* one of those books.

Instead, this book will change the way you think about what it means to *put your heart into what you're selling*. The philosophy in this book is the real game-changer: It's a shift in perspective, a leap of faith that many of the world's most successful leaders—in sales, in politics, in any business—have made. Now you can too.

What does it mean to have your heart in selling? It means living in an ethical and principled manner, of course. But more than that, it means genuinely caring about improving the lives and businesses of your customers. It means understanding human needs and behavior, and using that understanding to form an authentic connection, rather than trying to finesse a quick sale. It means leaving space to truly listen rather than bulldozing your way through a meeting. It means listening for the emotion behind the words—and caring about what you hear! Above all, it means *living* these principles in every aspect of your life.

If you are in a leadership position, selling with heart will increase job satisfaction among your management teams and sales forces. Teams that sell with heart are more open, more receptive, more engaged, and better able to let their passions and talents shine through.

The 10 Universal Truths: An Introduction

During the past 20 years, my colleagues and I have had the chance to work inside many Fortune 500 companies with enviable cultures and superior products. At the height of the market collapse, we helped fledgling real estate companies keep their doors open and regain their competitive edge. We have boosted call center revenue by teaching sales reps the psychology behind their scripts. Our training materials have improved the lives of hundreds of thousands of salespeople and young entrepreneurs—from new recruits to veterans wishing to master their game.

I've spent a lot of that time wondering why salespeople selling the same things and following the same processes can have such vastly different results. How can salespeople in the same auto dealership, real estate agents in the same marketplace, and sellers of similar software products produce such different outcomes? Why does one salesperson earn $50,000 per year, whereas another in the same industry earns $400,000?

Seeking answers to these questions, I made it my mission to study top sales leaders and salespeople in various industries.

For each person I studied, I asked myself: What did they say—and what *didn't* they say? How did they do it? Did they have secret tricks or best practices they could share?

It turns out that top salespeople have a lot of differences beyond the products they sell and the industries in which they work. Some are educated and some are streetwise; some are effusive, whereas others are shy. Some come from wealth, whereas others have struggled. But they are all the same in one important way.

Beyond knowing what to say and why to say it, the best salespeople know something else; something deeper, more penetrating, and more sustaining.

Talk to successful salespeople and you'll find that they have one thing in common. They not only lead with their hearts when connecting with others, they also connect deeply to themselves and their own goals and dreams. In other words, they know who they are and what they want out of life. Regardless of what they sell, where they live, or who their customers are, the best salespeople are authentic and filled with a sense of purpose.

This authenticity is more important than ever. If we as salespeople aren't coming from a place of integrity, customers know it instantly. Today's buyers, as I'm sure you'll agree, are savvier than ever, and they're wary of staged presentations and canned pitches. A recent Gallup poll found that customers consider salespeople such as real estate agents, auto dealers, and phone reps among the *least* ethical of all professions—only lobbyists and members of Congress ranked lower!

I've spent the majority of my career developing systems, models, and templates, but I'd never tell you that there's a one-size-fits-all method for sales. People are different and complex. Products are diverse. And markets are ever-changing. But though I don't believe in one-size-fits-all solutions, what I do know is this:

There are a few powerful principles about human behavior that apply to everyone, everywhere, every time. There are truths that help you not only connect with others, but also with yourself and your deeper purpose. They will not only help you do your job more effectively and authentically, they will also help you live a richer and more fulfilling life.

Top salespeople know how to balance heart and sales. They also understand that unless they really know themselves, they'll never truly connect with their customers—or anyone else, for that matter. They know that what you do matters, but *who you are* matters more.

These universal truths are all about achieving that balance, and more deeply connecting with your authentic self.

Please don't imagine that I've written this book because my life has been a parade of awards and victories or, conversely, struggle, failure, and pain. It's been an incredible and necessary combination of both. I've always lived my passion. I've always put my heart and soul into everything I've done. It hasn't always worked in my favor, but I don't have many regrets. My sincere hope is to help you find your purpose in life or, perhaps, reignite the passions that once propelled the choices you've already made.

Sales can be a tough game. It's full of rejection, stress, and self-doubt. But once your dreams are more potent than your fears, you will find that your rewards are far greater than your struggles.

This book and the 10 universal truths I'll share with you constitute a definitive guide to selling more and living with greater pride and purpose. I hope you find it provocative, funny, inspirational, authentic, and, above all, filled with heart.

The 10 Universal Truths

1. **Success starts with the growth equation.** Top salespeople share a willingness to take *responsibility* for their weaknesses, a deep *curiosity* about their customers and the world, and a desire for *mastery*. They commit to using what they've learned about their processes to continue improving. When you master this "growth equation" you will not only improve your sales record, you will transform your life.

2. **Emotions drive decision-making.** The desire to be loved, to create closeness, look good, feel good, be remembered—even to belong—drives all of our decision-making. Our ability to uncover our customer's emotional dominant motivators will dictate our success.

3. **Freedom lives in structure.** Pilots run through preflight check-lists. Free-throw shooters develop rituals to help them hit the same shot time and again. Bakers adhere to time-tested recipes. So why should it be different in sales? Highly successful sales-people have a process they follow and they follow that process every time. It may sound counterintuitive, but structure creates the freedom to act authentically and to create true connection.

4. **In sales, no never means no.** Are you paralyzed by fear? Good. Top salespeople know that the more fear they feel, the more important it is to tackle the fear. What you're afraid to do, you must do. The question you're afraid to ask, you must ask. In this chapter, we'll look at "getting out on the skinny branches." Failure is inevitable. Resilience is a life skill, one that will fill your soul and your pocket.

5. **Trust begins with empathy.** Trust is born of empathy, integrity, reliability, and competency. You need all four traits, but without connecting on an empathetic level, you won't have a chance

to demonstrate the other three. Empathy is the first building block of trust. We can't pretend to have empathy. Empathy is not about shifting the conversation to what you want to say or judging your customer. It's about being fully engaged and present to someone else's emotions.

6. **Integrity matters.** Once we cultivate true empathy, we find it impossible to lie to or cheat our customers—or anyone, for that matter, including ourselves. The word "sales" comes from the old English word for "give." When we sell, we must give. We can only maintain trust and enjoy enduring success when we cultivate honorable traits like reliability, competency, and integrity. Eventually, they become part of our character.

7. **Anything that can be told can be asked.** When we ask the right questions, we uncover what matters most. "Discovery questions" uncover customers' needs, direct their thinking down a path we choose, generate curiosity, and ultimately move them to action. These questions build rapport, gain commitment, and help your prospects sell themselves. Well-crafted questions help us make a point loudly, without having to raise our voice. Good questions create change. Great questions can change the world.

8. **Emotional commitment precedes economic commitment.** Most salespeople incorrectly assume that they can create a sense of urgency by threatening scarcity or appealing to greed. But if people don't want what you're selling, they won't care if there are only two left or whether you're throwing something else in. (Anyone want a stagecoach? It's on sale today only! And I'll throw in some horseshoes for free!) In this chapter, I'll discuss ways to engage customers with stories and build urgency by demonstrating how your product connects to precisely what motivates them.

9. **Removing resistance takes persistence.** As soon as a prospect displays resistance, most salespeople drop the price, modify the terms, or otherwise change the offer. But the truth is: only when someone is in a receptive emotional state can you close.

This section will include strategies for keeping customers receptive, isolating the toughest customer objections, and uncovering the real and final objection so you can close more deals more quickly.

10. **Looking for wrongs never makes you right.** Every day, in every encounter, you have a choice. You can look for what's right about that person or experience—what's valuable or productive—or you can look for what's wrong. When you're interacting with your associates or your customers, don't look for reasons why they won't buy. Look instead for reasons why they will buy. Whatever you look for, be certain you'll find it!

The Truth About Truths

After a large training event I presented a few years ago, an older man from the front row approached me and told me he'd been coming to my seminars for years.

"I've listened to all of your CDs," he said. "I watch your DVDs every week . . ."

I smiled, wondering what he was going to tell me. If a guy is watching and listening constantly to my work, I figured I was due for a big compliment, right?

Wrong.

"But I gotta tell you," he continued, "your training doesn't work."

I was shocked. I didn't know why he was telling me this or why he kept listening to my stuff if it wasn't working for him!

But I was curious. I asked him to tell me a bit about his process, and he described how he sold. I had to admit: He was a serious student of my work. (Heck, he knew my material better than I did.) It sounded as though he really grasped my approach to sales. He was saying all the right words and asking all the right questions.

Then I asked him to actually *show me* his presentation—and suddenly the problem was obvious.

Right from the start, it was clear that something was missing. He knew exactly what to say and do, yes, but something was interfering with his ability to execute everything properly. After we talked a little more, I got to the heart of the issue. It turned out that he didn't actually believe in his product and—even more importantly—he lacked compassion for his customers. It didn't matter what he was saying; he came across as inauthentic.

I encounter a lot of salespeople who are full of knowledge, but light on results, and I tell them what I told this man:

You can know something intellectually, but that doesn't mean you can execute it effectively.

I've been rock climbing for years. Before any climb, I study the route and learn all about the type of rock. But, believe me, once you're hanging from a rope at several hundred feet, knowing how to do something and actually doing it are two very different things. Yikes!

The only way any of us can improve our performance is by closing the gap between what we know and what we're actually doing.

You may have read the summary of the 10 Universal Truths and thought, "But I know all this. Of course I know I'm supposed to build trust, ask questions, and take responsibility."

But here's the tough question: Are you actually doing it? And are you doing it every time or maybe even most of the time?

If not, why not?

It turns out there's a very good reason.

Tackle Your Tendencies

Like other animals, humans fall into "default modes" when performing difficult or even life-preserving tasks. Think of these default modes as the path of least resistance: doing whatever takes the least amount of work or mental energy. The moose who visits our backyard doesn't veer far from the lush grassy patch. Why? It takes more effort to get food from elsewhere. The food is plentiful just where she is.

I first heard the term "default mode" in my Anusara yoga class. My instructor told the students that everyone has certain "tendencies." We default to these tendencies when we aren't hyper-focused. Why? Because they're easier. Our bodies naturally default to the easiest positions. We slouch our shoulders, or hang our head, or forget to breathe properly. When we're not really paying attention, we tend to slide into default mode. With time, in the workplace, these tendencies can lead to dramatic underperformance.

There's a hard science to explain why. Neuroscientists have discovered a part of the brain they call the "default mode network." It becomes hyperactive when we're in what's known as a "resting state."[1] (This is actually a good thing after work, during a break, or on weekends because this downtime refreshes the brain.)

Using this part of the brain can limit your abilities when interacting with a prospective customer, however. To truly connect, you must "wake up" out of this state. You must be fully present to sell with integrity and authenticity. Yet, somehow, this state of wakeful rest is where we all retreat to when we're distracted.

We all have default tendencies to overcome. These are the repetitive or destructive—and usually unconscious—behaviors that prohibit you from making a sale. Sometimes, when you're tired or distracted, they're more pronounced, but default mode takes over for several other reasons. I use the acronym "HELL" to sum them up.

Have You Fallen Into Sales HELL?

H = Habits
E = Ego
L = Lack of knowledge
L = Laziness

Habits

We default out of sheer habit. Many sales veterans are guilty of this. You've been doing something wrong for so long, you can't see how it wreaks havoc on your performance. Or the action is so subtle that you can't distinguish the behavior as a hindrance.

Charles Duhigg writes in *The Power of Habit* that when we repeatedly perform even mundane activities (such as brushing our teeth, brewing our morning coffee, or parallel parking) we form neurological patterns.[2] The more you repeat a behavior, the more you ingrain the habit. If you are unkind every day, you become an unkind person; if you don't listen to people, you become self-centered; when you empathize every day, you become empathetic. As the saying goes, we are what we repeatedly do. Good habits as well as bad ones get easier with time.

Habits are a natural part of being human. The problem, of course, is when we get stuck in bad habits that don't serve us. The good news is that bad habits can be changed—if we're aware of them. If we're disciplined about replacing old behaviors with new ones, we can change what we do and, ultimately, who we become.

Ego

According to research conducted by David Mayer and Herbert M. Greenberg, good salespeople have a need to conquer.[3] This particular type of ego drive gives us the ability to claim greatness, to say, "I'm going to be number one and earn a huge promotion."

But the other aspect of ego urges us to play the blame game and abdicate responsibility for a lost sale. An overblown ego keeps us from learning and growing as new technologies emerge or the client demands a different kind or level of interaction.

I've heard many salespeople excuse their poor performance by citing a recent study that shows the average attention span of people today has plummeted from 12 to 8 seconds.[4] They say goldfish have a longer attention span than people! If you don't believe me, go to the nearest pet store and have a staring contest with a goldfish. If you're like most people, my money's on the fish.

Here's the problem: Rather than owning up to their failure to hold a customer's attention, many salespeople make excuses for underperformance instead of finding ways to improve.

To paraphrase creative writing guru Robert McKee: You don't have a problem with attention span; you have a problem with "interest span."[5] It's not that our customers aren't paying attention. They just aren't paying attention to *us*. In other words, we aren't *holding* their attention. If you've ever binge-watched a TV series like *Mad Men, House of Cards*, or *Game of Thrones*, I'm sure you'll agree that you pay closer attention to the episodes than you would to, say, your sock drawer. When you sell, are you Kevin Spacey in *House of Cards* or are you about as intriguing as a mismatched set of socks? Don't let your ego rob you of your ability to take responsibility for your performance!

As long as I'm going all Dr. Phil on you, here's another question: When you lose a sale, do you look for ways you could have done your job better? Or are you quick to blame external circumstances? How willing are you to look at the habits that are holding you back?

Lack of Knowledge

This might be the most common reason newer salespeople succumb to their negative tendencies: *They simply don't know any better.* Perhaps they haven't learned the steps of their sales process, haven't mastered their product knowledge, or don't have enough experience overcoming and isolating common objections.

Is a lack of product or market knowledge the fault of the manager or the salesperson? Sometimes it's hard to determine where one person's responsibility ends and another's begins, but top performers know that if they lack knowledge, they had better seek that knowledge. If you're not getting enough information from your manager, ask questions. Seek out information from other sources. Refuse to become complacent. You were not born to be average.

Don't think for a moment that you can blame your lack of success on the fact that you aren't a "born salesperson." As the late, great sales trainer and motivator Zig Ziglar said, "I looked in the paper this morning and a bunch of salespeople died, but I didn't see a single salesperson born."[6]

Are great salespeople born or made? Neither. Great salespeople are salespeople who commit to overcome their negative tendencies to make themselves great.

LAZINESS

When I speak of laziness, I don't mean we'd rather be lying on a deck chair drinking a margarita (although we might) or watching reruns of *Leave it to Beaver* and *My Three Sons*. Rather, I'm referring to the lazy moments when we aren't purposefully engaged, when we aren't bringing our "A-game."

None of us are immune to the lure of laziness. How many times have you made promises like, "I'm going to work out in the morning," "I'm not drinking tonight," or, "I'm calling five referrals today"—only to default into a justification for why you'll start tomorrow?

But chronic laziness can really take its toll. A colleague of mine—let's call her Karen—sleeps until nine every morning and leaves the office at five, and for the last 20 years has been telling me: "Levitin, you live to work. I, on the other hand, work to live."

Karen has rules—lots of them. She refuses to take extra shifts, or respond to customers who need servicing, or seek advice from a mentor. As a result, Karen lives paycheck to paycheck. Whenever we meet she tells me, "If I had your money, I'd burn mine. You're so lucky."

I don't tell her that luck had little to do with it. I also don't tell her that I had to train myself to avoid procrastination and commit to staying focused even when I wanted to check out. Why don't I tell her any of those things? Because she is too deeply committed to her own mediocrity to hear what I have to say.

Salespeople that default out of laziness fail to prepare for client meetings, take shortcuts in their sales processes, and often go on the defensive when a customer voices an objection. The customer isn't attacking the salesperson, but laziness can cause us to take innocent statements as personal affronts. The customer is just trying to learn something. If he learns that you're too impatient to answer his questions, you're also teaching him to go buy from someone else.

Mediocre salespeople have another vice: They're addicted to what they call multitasking. They constantly check their e-mail, Facebook, and Twitter accounts under the guise of multitasking, even though science has shown us there's really no such thing. According to best-selling author and neuroscientist Dan Levitin (I'm his proud sister), "Multitasking is a diabolical illusion. When people think they're multitasking, they're actually just switching from one task to another rapidly. Even though we're getting a lot done, ironically, multitasking makes us demonstrably less efficient."[7]

Why? Because we're diverting our precious and limited attention away from what matters most (the customers!) to what matters less (what your sister posted about her breakfast on her Cabo vacation yesterday).

If you're not performing at the level you'd like to be, ask yourself whether you're really *paying attention* to your customers and your work—or whether you're slipping off into a fantasy world and filling your downtime with activities that sap your energy.

We blame our customers for not paying attention, but who just lost the staring contest with the goldfish?

If you've ever found yourself in sales HELL, congratulations! You're human. Falling into default-mode behaviors is a natural part of being alive, and it's probably impossible to ever completely eliminate these tendencies.

However, our goal is to bring our heart into the sales process, to go beyond mere interaction, and really connect with customers. Remember: Not only does this make us more effective salespeople, it also increases our satisfaction in every area of our lives. Default-mode behaviors rip us out of the present moment—and it's only in the present moment that we can have the most impact and experience the most joy.

What Are Your Default Tendencies?

Now, be brutally honest with yourself. What are *your* default-mode behaviors? Here's a short list to get your brain going (for a full list of default behaviors that correspond to each universal truth, go to ShariLevitin.com):

* Hearing a customer problem, and immediately trying to solve it rather than uncovering *why* it's a problem.
* Giving the customer way too much information.
* Selling features that aren't important to the customer.
* Talking too much during the discovery or closing process.
* Not involving all of the decision-makers.
* Making your offer sound too good to be true.
* Exaggerating product benefits . . . just this once.
* Telling the customer how your product works, instead of sharing with them how they'll *feel* when they use, own, or engage with your product.
* Not preparing ahead of time and just sort of winging it.
* Telling the customer that their existing choices, partners, or way of doing something are all wrong, just so your solution sounds superior.

And then there's the biggest default of them all:

* *Not listening or working to uncover the customer's emotional motivators in the first place!*

Now, ask yourself: Which tendencies am I most prone to? And when I do fall into default mode, what part of sales HELL am I usually stuck in: habit, ego, lack of knowledge, or laziness?

Having a basic understanding of your tendencies is going to help you get the most out of this book and so, right now, set aside time to think about what default mode looks like to you. After all, until we're willing to admit we have a problem, we certainly can't solve it.

Your turn—make a list of the destructive tendencies you'd like to abandon.

Now that you know the true source of your sales struggles, it's time to see what you can start doing about it. You'll find those surprising answers in the next chapter.

*Names and identifying details of many of the people and companies that appear in the book have been changed to protect their privacy.

CHAPTER 1

Success Starts With the Growth Equation

Universal Truth #1: Top salespeople share a willingness to take *responsibility* for their weaknesses, a deep *curiosity* about their customers and the world, and a desire for *mastery*. They commit to using what they've learned about their processes to continue improving. When you master this "growth equation" you will not only improve your sales record, you will transform your life.

When I was about 30, I heard about a sales opportunity at Marriott. Fortunately, I was hired, because it was there that I met my first sales mentor.

Motivational speaker and author Marcus Buckingham, formerly with the Gallup Organization, once said, "People don't leave jobs, they leave managers."[1] As for me, I stayed and thrived with Marriott because of one man: Greg Willingham.

Greg grew up in the land business and was what Bostonians call "wicked smaht." It was because of Greg that I was able to rise through the ranks at Marriott, eventually becoming the top salesperson and going on to help lead the top sales team in the company.

That didn't mean working for Greg was easy—far from it. There was no messing around in his salesroom. Sales meetings started every morning at 8:00 a.m. sharp. If you weren't in your seat, you got no customers that day. That's right, not one lead. The reason for your tardiness didn't matter. One day, a company bulldozer rammed into my colleague's Subaru while he was pulling into the parking lot.

No leads.

Greg wasn't interested in reasons. "I hire the best salespeople I can find," he said. "I don't want to spend my time listening to excuses."

Greg taught me the most valuable lesson of my career—the three goals of any sales encounter:

1. Make the customer feel better about you and your company than they did before you met.
2. Make a sale.
3. If the customer doesn't buy, find out the real reason. Learn from it, accept responsibility, and don't make the same mistake again.

It's the third rule that I've found to be the most important and, often, the most painful. The moment you really start to take *responsibility* for your actions, you will feel the pain of failures more acutely than before. But you will also learn from each experience so you'll never make the same mistakes again.

This willingness to look at your mistakes requires *curiosity*. The most successful people I've encountered aren't afraid to say, "Yes, I messed up, but what did I do wrong? What's the lesson? How can I get better?" They know they might not win back a lost sale or fix a mistake, but they do commit to changing their behavior next time.

How? By taking a good look at their habits and by being vulnerable enough to admit what's working and what isn't. The willingness to learn and grow is what leads to true *mastery*.

The Growth Equation

Responsibility, curiosity, and mastery make up what I refer to as the growth equation—and top performers understand and practice this universal truth.

Why is a commitment to growth such a necessary component of selling with heart? Because when we take responsibility, we draw people in rather than pushing them away. Increased curiosity creates more authentic relationships. By mastering sales techniques, you will live in the moment with your customers and be present to their needs and emotions.

Work on all three of these things and your connections will be deeper and your paycheck will be bigger. Of course, you have to first believe that this kind of growth is even possible.

Make a commitment to growth—and surround yourself with others who've done the same.

For years I thought that sales skills were either something you were born with or not. I figured that my talents, much like my frizzy black hair, were facts of life.

In her bestselling book, *Mindset: The New Psychology of Success*, Stanford Business School professor Carol Dweck presents a powerful way of looking at success. High achievers possess more than intelligence and talent. In addition, they all have a commitment to growth and continual learning.

Dweck says that people have either one of two types of "mindsets" that have a powerful impact on how they conduct their lives.[2] The first group of people—those with a *fixed* mindset—believe that their qualities and abilities are static. They think there's a limit to their basic talents and nothing can change that. As a result, they feel a deep urgency to prove themselves to others.

We all know people stuck in a fixed mindset. They say things like:

* I'm not good at math.
* I don't remember people's names.
* I'm not a natural salesperson.
* I don't do technology.
* I'm not interested in politics!
* No one finds me attractive.
* I'm not the athletic type.

Because those with fixed mindsets aren't curious to learn more and often don't put in the effort to become masters in their fields; they hide behind false bravado. They try to mask their deficiencies, instead of trying to overcome them.

People with *growth* mindsets, on the other hand, believe that their basic qualities "are things you can cultivate through toil and persistence."[3] These people are energized by learning and invigorated by overcoming failure. To them, life is a journey of gathering new information, making new connections, asking for constructive feedback, and learning from painful lessons.

A passion for stretching themselves is the hallmark of those with a growth mindset.

A perfect example of someone with a growth mindset was Benjamin Franklin. The consistent theme in Franklin's life was self-improvement. As the brother of seven, and the child of a poor candle maker, he had less than two years of formal education and yet he became one of the wealthiest, most respected intellectuals of the 18th century.[4]

From an early age, Franklin read everything he could. He loved the knowledge he found in books and in 1727 formed a club called the Junto, a structured forum to discuss and debate intellectual and worldly topics with fellow club members.

Learning about the world was obviously important to Franklin—but so was spending time with other thinkers and community leaders who were as curious and committed to learning as he was.

Think for a moment about the people you surround yourself with: Are they people who inspire you and fuel your energy, or do they just suck the life out of you?

My (former) friend Cindy always had a health issue, a problem with her ex-husband, or a gripe about her mother. I somehow became her sounding board and her bartender, listening to her sob stories over too many bottles of wine. Alas, Cindy would never do anything about her situation. She preferred complaining to therapy, and victimization to optimization. When I finally realized there was nothing I could do to help her until she started to help herself, we parted ways.

The next time you find yourself feeling stuck in a fixed mindset, think about what you might do to step outside yourself and learn from your mistakes. Think about those colleagues and friends who strive for improvement, and ask yourself if you're spending enough time helping each other grow.

This commitment to growth and the bonds you form with other growth-minded colleagues will pave the way for you to master the growth equation.

Responsibility

At one of my consulting workshops, I kicked off the first morning by greeting each salesperson by name. They all replied with the same good cheer.

All but one.

Instead of saying hello, Linda was quick to make excuses as to why she wasn't having any luck with the previous day's assignments.

"The prospects are terrible," she said. "They don't buy."

The second morning, it was the same thing.

"Good morning," I called out. "What a grand day!"

But it was never a grand day for Linda.

"These leads are NQs!" she hissed. (NQ is short for "not qualified.")

Who does that, I wondered. Who blames everyone and everything but themselves for their lack of sales?

Actually, a lot of people do. Many salespeople blame external circumstances for their lack of success. But when we do this, we erode our own power.

We've all met chronic blamers—reactive people who limit their ability to take control of their lives. Reactive salespeople are easy to spot. They use phrases such as:

* I can't help it.
* They didn't have the money.
* It's marketing's fault.
* I don't have the time.
* I never get any support.

Often, chronic blamers are fearful about their job security—and for good reason. Take Linda, for example. Her organization had more than 500 salespeople who all worked together at the same office. Every month they had awards for the top three salespeople. Linda had never been close to the top; in fact, she was always in the bottom 10.

But an interesting thing happened during the course of the seminar. The techniques I was sharing resonated with Linda and, just two weeks later, she went from number 125 on her team to number two. Around the time the awards were announced, I noticed Linda in the back of the room on a little brown chair, writing feverishly on a yellow pad.

I asked her what she was doing.

"Writing my speech," she said. "I'm going to share with everyone what I did to win the number two slot."

I congratulated Linda for improving her sales record, but I also told her what I tell salespeople all over the world:

We can't take the glory for being great if we won't take the responsibility when we're not.

Remember: Linda wasn't blaming herself for being number 125—she was blaming the customers. So although I was thrilled to congratulate her for her victory, I warned her that she needed to be equally willing to take responsibility the next time customers weren't buying.

Top salespeople never blame external factors for their lack of success. They know that, even as a veteran, you can go from having a great month where everyone's buying to one where you can't sell anyone anything. You try everything, but you can't even talk your dog into going for a walk. As Eric Greitens writes in his book *Resilience*, "While fear can be your friend, excuses are almost always your enemy. Faced with a choice between hard action and easy excuses people often choose the excuse. . . . Excellence is difficult. An excuse is seductive."[5]

People who sell from the heart never blame external factors for their lack of success. They hold themselves accountable and, as a result, they consistently improve.

You can have the greatest sales system in the world, but if you won't take responsibility for your own success, in the end, it won't matter.

When Organizations Play the Blame Game

If the failure to take responsibility can prevent an otherwise talented salesperson from growing, it can mean the death of an organization. Yet, in too many companies, the blame game runs rampant. A single chronic blamer can turn an entire culture into a game of finger pointing and "It's your fault, not mine" thinking.

A few years ago, I sat with a group of senior leaders who weren't meeting their quotas. They were struggling to get salespeople to prospect correctly and to isolate objections.

I met with the leadership team separately and asked them to identify what they saw as the major issue.

"The salespeople just don't listen," they complained. "We tell them over and over again what to do and it goes in one ear and out the other."

"Really?" I said. I was shocked. "Who's in charge of training here?"

There was an awkward silence.

"We are," one of them responded.

"They're looking to you for leadership and direction," I said. "They rely on *you* to provide mentorship and accountability! And *you're* blaming *them?*"

Next, I met with the sales team. Their biggest beef with management was that they weren't providing enough support or guidance about how to close.

"It's their fault," they complained.

Really? Doesn't anybody in this company want to accept some responsibility? Apparently not.

No matter where you sit in an organization, blaming others is always a bad idea, not simply because it alienates people, because it's lazy, or because it robs you of respect. There's a deeper reason—one that won't just cause short-term problems, but will destroy your organization's chance at long-term growth:

Blaming other people and external circumstances prevents you from learning, and it prevents your company from growing.

You can start to take more responsibility immediately by changing your self-talk and the questions you ask yourself. Consider the following alternatives to some old standby excuses:

- **"They didn't have the money."** Instead, think about where you could have improved. For example, "I didn't show them the value. Did I find a problem? Was it big enough?"
- **"They're indecisive."** Maybe, but what could *you* have done differently? "I didn't make enough of a connection. What else could I have done to build trust?"
- **"Someone gave them a better deal."** Instead of blaming your competitors, keep your focus on you. "I didn't differentiate our offering. What are the power statements I could have used to better differentiate my offer?"

Despite years of training myself to take responsibility, I still find myself asking accusatory questions like "Who took my car keys?" or "Who left the milk out?" My default mechanism is often to blame. I sometimes think that's why I seek advice from so many people when I'm going through rough times. That way if the advice doesn't pan out, I can abdicate responsibility. I'm not proud of this, but I am certainly aware of it.

The truth is that it's easier to blame than it is to accept criticism. Here's how to catch yourself in the act. If someone asks you why something went wrong, do you start a sentence with the words "He," "She," or "They"? The very use of those words suggests that someone else, somewhere else, is in control. The sales gods must be against you!

As soon as you say "I," you've taken back control for your failures—and your successes.

Curiosity

Years ago, the manager of a European conglomerate asked me to help out a struggling new salesperson. Buzzcut Bruce, we called him. Now, Bruce was new to sales. It turns out he excelled as a private investigator in Louisiana, but after having just moved to Colorado he thought he'd take a whack at a career in fractional real estate sales.

Whenever I coach a new salesperson, I focus on the discovery questions they ask their clients. Bruce asked the right questions all right, but his questioning quickly deteriorated into interrogations. Not a good idea. Here's an example:

"So Charlotte, you just mentioned your last holiday in Montana," Bruce would ask. "Do you and Brad always vacation in the summer?"

"Yes," the prospect would reply. "That's when the kids are out of school."

"And what month do you travel?" he'd ask.

"Usually August. It gets pretty hot in Texas, so we like to head north."

Painful pause . . .

"Hmmmm . . . but you said that Christmas is when you take the most frequent breaks. So which is it, ma'am?"

Yikes.

I couldn't tell if he was trying to get a signature on a contract or a confession.

Now, this is an extreme example of what not to do. Not every novice salesperson is going to grill their prospects as hard as a former private eye. But my point is this: Unless salespeople are truly curious, the discovery process may *feel* like an interrogation to customers.

I've watched thousands of salespeople go through the motions of asking the right questions, only to completely annoy their customers along the way. Why? Because they display a lack of genuine curiosity. When objections arise, instead of asking questions that will put the customer at ease and create a connection, they go on the defensive. It's not enough to ask questions; you actually have to listen for the answers!

As an alternative approach, I love the quote from the book *Just Listen* by Mark Goulston and repeat it to my son frequently: "Be more interested than interesting."[6] The more you listen, the smarter people think you are. Why start talking and louse up their positive impression of you?

The Five Attributes of Curious People

Consider some of the habits of truly curious salespeople:

* They ask questions that help them better understand their customers—not simply those that allow them to elbow in their point of view.
* They do their homework before they meet a prospect. Who is this person? How long has he or she been with the company? (What they don't do is prejudge.)
* They dig deep in order to find out what really matters to their customers at the heart level.
* They want to get to know their customers' inner worlds and discover how it affects their outer worlds.
* Instead of reacting negatively, they seek to understand why a prospect might be putting off a decision.

Curious neuroscientists are studying the brain to uncover the neurological impact of, you guessed it, curiosity. Some of the most recent findings support a theory developed by Carnegie-Mellon's George Loewenstein known as the "information gap."

"According to Loewenstein, curiosity is rather simple," writes Jonah Lehrer in *Wired*. "It comes when we feel a gap 'between what we know and what we want to know.' This gap has emotional consequences: it feels like a mental itch, a mosquito bite on the brain. We seek out new knowledge because that's how we scratch the itch."[7]

So what does all of this have to do with increasing your paycheck?

As it turns out, lots.

A Ferrari on Crap Gas

The first real fight between my husband and me took place in a coffee shop. I don't remember exactly what we were eating or what time of day it was— just that the place was far from chic, and two groups of college students sat uncomfortably close to us. I also recall my husband telling me, "You're a Ferrari on crap gas."

What the hell did that mean? I wasn't sure, but I could tell it wasn't a compliment.

"You're very smart," he said, "but you know nothing about the world. You don't read. You don't even know who Nelson Mandela was, for god's sake!"

Yankees center fielder. Everyone knows that.

Okay, nobody's *that* dumb. I told him I did know, but I had forgotten—a typical response from me. Of course, that didn't work this time.

"I'm running a company," I said. "I'm learning social media marketing and studying leadership." I justified my lack of breadth by hiding behind the "Hotel Theory of Learning"—an idea I'd heard that boils down to "Before something can check in, something else has to check out." I was quite pleased with myself when I explained to him that I have *so* much new knowledge that there just wasn't enough room for the old knowledge.

He didn't buy it.

"I want to talk to my wife about something other than sales."

The truth is he was right. And instead of arguing with him, I decided to listen for once. I began reading the newspaper, the *New Yorker*, fiction, and nonfiction. I started paying attention to politics. I read about economic developments in the United States and abroad. I paid attention to conflicts going on in other countries. This allowed me to build rapport with a greater number of people as well as to interact with higher-end clients.

I also found out that Nelson Mandela didn't play center field.

He was a shortstop.

As my world grew, so did my relationships, my self-esteem, and my business. Today, I can't imagine life without op-ed columns, classic fiction, TED Talks, and the whole world of current information that is mine for the taking.

To be curious about the complexities of the world we live in is an essential part of being an engaged citizen and an interesting person. It's also become more important than ever for salespeople to be tuned in to what's going on in the wider world.

When I began my career in the early 1980s, the salesperson was the only channel the customer had when it came to getting information about a product. The customer either believed me or not. Oh, sure, a couple of decades ago people could ask their Uncle Archie if he had ever used our product, but it was up to me to build or destroy the trust between me and the customer.

By contrast, today's customers have countless ways to receive information about the product they're considering. No longer must they rely on the salesperson's explanations or printed materials. They can conduct their own research, watch video demos, scour through hundreds of Yelp reviews—you name it.

As a result, today's salespeople need to be so much more than just our sales pitches.

Today, you must be at least as educated as your customer. Knowledge is necessary for credibility—and I'm not just talking about knowing about your product and those of your competitors. You need to know the news of the day and how it might be shaping the moods and emotions of your customers. You must understand economic trends and how they might be affecting people's confidence about making major purchases.

My good friend Eric White employs 400 salespeople in his business in Mexico. He suggests to each of them to read news like the *Wall Street Journal* or the *New York Times* daily. "How can we possibly ask our American customers to pay $25,000 to $750,000 for our product," he says, "if we don't understand their politics, their business, and their economy?"[8]

I can't argue with that.

PUT IT INTO ACTION

Amp Up Your Curiosity

If you're looking to amp up your own curiosity, ask yourself the following questions:

* Do I read the news and engage with challenging material or relevant nonfiction daily? (Simply watching TV doesn't count!)

* Do I know as much about my product or service as my most educated customer?
* Do I take courses online, participate in discussion groups, and share valuable content with others?
* Do I learn new technologies? When I can't figure something out, do I shut down, or do I ask for help?
* Do I surround myself with those that have different opinions than my own?

If the answer to any of those questions is "no," the work you have to do is clear. But I hesitate to call it "work." So many of us associate learning about the world with passing (or failing) tests. The great thing about continuing our education as adults is that we get to choose what to study.

You don't have to know everything, but knowing what interests you, what fascinates you, what keeps you engaged—and what interests, fascinates, and engages your customers—is a great place to start.

Mastery

A few years ago, the Portuguese pianist Maria João Pires arrived at Amsterdam's Royal Concertgebouw ready to play a Mozart concerto.

But the second the music began, a look of horror appeared on the acclaimed musician's face.

"She was shocked because she was expecting us to play another concerto," said conductor Riccardo Chailly in a video that went viral a few years ago. "She kind of jumped and panicked like an electric shock."[9]

Can you imagine how she must have felt? There she was on stage in front of a huge audience, and she had prepared to play the wrong piece.

But after realizing her mistake, an amazing thing happened. Pires was able to play the piece she had not prepared to play, completely from memory. The audience never knew the difference. Neither did the orchestra.

Unconscious Mastery

Mastery is taking a step beyond just being great. Mastery means you're so accomplished, like Maria João Pires, that you can perform your craft without thinking about the details while doing it, even under awkward or adverse conditions.

What does this level of mastery allow you to do? Everything that's critical for a top salesperson. Because you're not hung up on thinking about what to say next, or how to answer a concern accurately, you are freed up to:

* Listen with your heart.
* Listen for the emotion behind the words.
* Pivot when the customer throws you a curve ball.
* Change your strategy when an unexpected event occurs (you prepare the wrong slide show, only one decision-maker shows up, the global economy collapses, you break a heel).
* Teach it to others.

Although time and practice are obviously key to become a master, I've found there are some ways to jumpstart your pursuit of greatness:

* Seek feedback.
* Give up your ego.
* Repeat.

These steps are not something you do once and then forget about. Mastery is an ongoing process of taking on new challenges, being humble enough to learn from your mistakes, and persisting.

Feedback Will Help Power Your Performance

I used to work with a guy I'll call Barry. (That's not his real name. His real name was Sam.) Barry showed up to an interview with the boss, carrying his trophies and plaques in his suitcase. He placed them on his desk before the meeting started. Barry was a skilled presenter, but he wasn't interested in improvement.

Barry was his own worst enemy. When his sales went down, his excuses went up. He spent more time defending his lack of sales than it would have taken to learn more about his product and market. When offered coaching, Barry pointed to his awards and said he didn't need any. Soon, Barry's trophies were a relic of a decade that had long past. As the expression goes, nothing recedes like success.

When someone doesn't accept valuable feedback, that person cannot grow. Eventually, Barry's complaints about everything from the lamb chops he ate the night before to the company's lack of training destroyed his relationships and his chance at growth. (Have you ever noticed that it's the top 25 percent of the salespeople who buy sales aids such as books and online learning programs? You may say, "Well, it's because they can afford it." I can tell you firsthand it's the other way around: They can afford to finance their ongoing education because they've been putting in the investment since day one.)

Learning isn't just something you do with books, CDs, or online programs. Working with mentors is also key to achieving higher levels of performance. Your brain needs to know what's working and what isn't so it can improve. Online training is great—I offer a ton of it—but it's not sufficient. You need feedback from a living human being so you know specifically where you need to improve. Feedback is just as hard to give as it is to receive, but it's an essential part of learning. I recommend finding a mentor, as I did, who is competent, dependable, and driven to help facilitate your growth and provide real-time feedback.

Whether you're a skier, author, or parent, research shows that positive, immediate, and constructive feedback will help you understand what you're doing well and what you're doing poorly so you can practice, repeat, and master your best behavior. Otherwise, you're just grooving bad habits deeper into your brain until you can do a terrible job without even having to think about it!

PUT IT INTO ACTION

Become a Master at Receiving Feedback

* **Make certain that the person who's giving you the feedback understands what you're trying to accomplish.** Think about the iconic quote from Harper Lee's novel *To Kill a Mockingbird*: "You never really understand a person until you consider things from his point of view—until you climb inside of his skin and walk around in it."[10] Don't assume that the person giving you feedback will automatically know what you want to achieve. Letting him or her know a bit about your goals will help ensure you get the *right* feedback.

* **Seek out someone who can give you constructive feedback.** This is hard. No one likes being told what they did wrong. The person who offers feedback is wise to first tell you what you did right. By hearing the good stuff first, our brains will be more receptive to the areas where we need to improve. In fact, a *Harvard Business Review* study confirms that individuals who receive at least a 6–1 ratio of positive-to-negative advice significantly outperform those who are more often criticized.[11] In short, find a mentor who gently tells you how to improve and who recognizes your strengths.

* **Only focus on a maximum of three things at a time.** The brain can't possibly remember 36 new things to incorporate into a sales presentation. In golf, there's an expression called the "swing thought." The idea is that when you're about to make an important shot, you don't have time to remember 12 different things. So a good swing coach will offer just one thing to recall, and that one key piece of guidance triggers all the other things you know to do. It's the same thing in sales.

* **Feedback must be specific.** In seminars I've taught around the world, I've heard countless salespeople proclaim that they want to be more successful. What does that mean? It obviously means different things to different people. To some, success might be earning $25,000 per month and buying a new BMW. To others, it may mean getting a promotion, having time to do charity work, or spending more time with family. Again, being clear about what you're trying to achieve will help you get the specific feedback you need.

What Are You Willing to Give Up?

Although the advice I've given in this chapter might seem simple and clear, that doesn't mean it's easy. Accepting responsibility, learning from our failures, asking for constructive criticism—none of this stuff is easy.

For many of us, the tendency to blame everyone but ourselves goes very deep. When we're children, we learn that if we can take the blame off ourselves, we can avoid punishment and escape our parents' anger. Unless we're lucky enough to have learned about the value of constructive criticism and honest self-assessment, many of us carry this behavior into adulthood.

I want to share one last story about how my mentor Greg helped me get comfortable with this process early on in my career:

One day, I stood with him on the balcony of our sales office. The trees were full of the previous night's frost, the clouds dark and undecided.

"What's your goal for the New Year?" Greg asked me.

"$100,000," I said. "I'm going to be number one in the company *and* I'm going to buy a white BMW."

"Wow. $100,000?" he said. (Keep in mind this was 1987, so that would translate into about a half a million today.) "Well, what did you make last year?"

"$33,000."

"And the year before?"

"$29,050."

He looked at me and scratched his head. "Let me get this right," he said. "Just because you're with a different company, selling a different product, you think all of a sudden you're going to triple your income?"

Suddenly, I wasn't so sure of myself. "Here's the deal, Shari," he said. "In order to get something that you've never had before, you have to give something up. So, what are you willing to give up?"

I thought about it for a moment. "I don't know," I said.

"Well, go home and think about it," he said.

It didn't take long for me to come up with an answer. Every night, at 6 on the dot, my colleagues and I would go to the Jackalope Bar for drinks. We were young and had all the answers, so discussions surrounded how much better things would be if we were in charge.

I realized that all our talk wasn't getting any of us closer to running the company. If I really wanted to get better, I needed more training.

When I told Greg my plan to trade in the Jackalope for sober evenings at home reading books by Tom Hopkins, he said, "Great. That's a start. That will get you to about $45,000. What else can you give up?"

That night, I thought some more. I knew of only two ways to make more money in sales: more training or more customers.

I returned to Greg's office with my plan.

"Excellent," he said. "That will get you to about $55,000. But there's one more thing you have to give up if you want to succeed."

I didn't know if I had anything else to give, but I wasn't going to back down now, so I asked him to tell me.

"Well, I've watched you for a while and it's going to be the hard," he said. "I don't know if you have it in you."

How dare he say that, I thought? I can do anything I put my mind to. (That's what my mother always said, anyway.)

He looked at me and, after a few moments, he said, "You have to give up your ego."

I let that sink in as he continued.

"There are two kinds of ego: good ego and bad ego," he said. "Good ego gives you the ability to claim greatness. It's your good ego that says, 'I'm going to be number one in my company and I'm going to buy a BMW.'

"Then there's the bad ego," he said. "Salespeople with bad ego blame everybody when things aren't going right, they defend their positions rather than accepting feedback, and they choose complacency over mastery."

I listened to what Greg had told me, and by the end of 1994, I had made $108,000. I bought a brand-new, white BMW.

I wish I could tell you that I've abandoned my bad ego for good, but every once in a while it rears its ugly head. In fact, it's one of my worst default behaviors.

What I do know is that paying attention to whether my ego is out of whack is just like every other aspect of the growth equation. It's a process: one that we must repeat, practice, and eventually master. The rewards are endless.

CHAPTER 2

Emotions Drive Decision-Making

Universal Truth #2: The desire to be loved, to create closeness, look good, feel good, be remembered— even to belong—drives all of our decision-making. Our ability to uncover our customer's emotional dominant motivators will dictate our success.

Saving Lives or Saving Money?

Tim never pictured himself in sales. He'd earned his helicopter pilot's license in New York, his commercial pilot's license in Michigan, and he'd graduated from nursing school in Seattle. He had flown hundreds of patients per year to emergency rooms by medical helicopter. He was proud of his work saving lives.

But Tim was frustrated: Competitors in the medevac business were crushing his business.

"How do I convince hospitals that our flight program is better than the competition?" he asked me. "We're cheaper. In fact, we charge *38 percent less!*"

Tim was so convinced of the incredible value he offered, that he pitched his services solely on price savings.

After he told me this, I paused.

"Do you have any children?" I asked him.

"Yes," he said. "My son is 11."

"Imagine getting a phone call. It's terrible news. Your son has suffered a snowboarding accident," I said. "It's life-threatening. In the moment you receive that call from Ski Patrol, do you care at all about the price of emergency helicopter transport?"

"Absolutely not," he replied.

"Neither do your customers," I told him. "They care about one thing: saving lives. You're focusing on the wrong benefit. What's the real metric hospitals use to judge medical helicopter companies?"

"Survival rate," he told me.

"Perfect," I said. "So what is your company's survival rate compared to your competition's?"

"It's a million times better."

"Really!" I exclaimed. "How come? What makes the difference for you guys?"

"We have much better medical practitioners," he assured me. "We're farther away, so it takes a little longer for us to arrive at the scene. But the quality of care we provide more than makes up for the slight difference in arrival time."

Tim told me a story about a high-school boy who was recently in an accident.

"The competitor's equipment broke down," he said. "So we transferred the boy to our helicopter. We had to resuscitate him three times on the way to the hospital. But he arrived alive. We returned him to his family three days later."

He continued, "Two weeks went by. I was sitting in a Starbucks when a middle-aged woman recognized me and broke into tears. She said, 'You . . . you saved Brandon's life.'"

After a bit of coaching, Tim changed his presentation. Instead of talking about price, he focused on the emotional benefits of using his company.

He didn't shy away from asking customers a very straightforward question: "What's more important to you in choosing a provider: speed of arrival or number of lives saved?"

I spoke to Tim a month after our session. He'd just landed the biggest contract in his company's history. How? He'd simply asked the right questions and told the story of saving the high-school student.

Make the Invisible Visible

Once you understand what drives your customers, sales becomes much easier. Urgency is created by desire, not price breaks and manufactured pressure. But here's the tricky part: *These desires are often hidden.* They're subconscious or invisible.

Your job as a salesperson is to make the invisible visible.

The Emotional Brain

A few years ago, neuroscientist Antonio Damasio revealed a groundbreaking discovery.

People with damage in the emotion-generating part of the brain, he noted, not only couldn't feel emotions like love, jealousy, or pride, they also couldn't make decisions.[1] They couldn't even make insignificant decisions like choosing between a hamburger and a chicken salad.

The rational mind cannot make decisions without involving the emotional mind.

We buy for emotional reasons, not simply logical ones. In my seminars, I ask participants to draw two columns. On the left, they write down their last major purchase—for example, a car, home, piece of jewelry, and so on. In the right column, they write *why they believe* they purchased it.

At first, the responses are predictably simplistic. For instance, a young man in my seminar told me he purchased a new Louis Vuitton briefcase because he needed something to hold his papers in. I asked why he didn't just purchase a backpack if he was simply seeking something to carry his stuff.

"They're more economical," I told him.

After a bit of banter, he cracked a smile and admitted that he traveled frequently. "I want to be treated with respect," he said. "Like I'm *somebody*."

Next, a man named Mario claimed he purchased his father's Italian restaurant for the investment potential. After several more questions, he shared his deep need to impress his father. His dad never did believe in him. Mario would prove him wrong.

We all make these emotional decisions whether we realize it or not. I don't blame these men for believing that they prized logic over emotion. After all, I don't tell most people why I redecorated my home 15 years ago.

"There was a great sale over at Elegante Furnishings," I told my pals when they asked me about my new decor.

But in truth, only my best friend Colleen and the sales clerk at Elegante knew the real reason I had invested in hardwood floors, an overstuffed couch, and the latest trends in artwork.

I had wandered into Elegante heartbroken, ashamed, and lonely. All I wanted was a long-burning spruce candle to rid my home of the smell of divorce. If I could have found one on my own, I never would have talked to a salesperson. Then I met Torrey, a rock star salesperson. Just by asking questions—and listening to me, and I really mean *listening* to me—she found out *why* I really wanted the candle.

We salespeople think we're so tough, but we're really putty in the hands of a pro. An hour later, Torrey had helped me redesign my home—and, more importantly, re-create my life. If Torrey had only asked me what I *wanted* that day, she'd have made commission on a $20 candle. Instead, she uncovered my *core motivation* for buying—and sold me $40,000 worth of furnishings. (She threw in the candle.)

Before we really dive into this chapter, I want to take a moment and offer some clarity of definitions. I will be using the terms "core motivators," "Third-Level motivators," "emotional motivators," and "dominant buying motives" interchangeably. A recent *Harvard Business Review* (*HBR*) piece called them "high-impact motivators."[2] They all mean the same thing: the deeper emotional reasons that ultimately drive a person to a decision. (Later, I will refer to this idea as WIFM, meaning the customer needs to know, "What's in it for me?")

How can you, like Torrey, get to the heart of your customers' core motivators?

Master the Seven Core Motivators

Human beings are more alike than we are different. We all yearn for deeper connection. We all want more time and less stress. We all desire health and well-being, freedom, adventure, revitalization, and self-improvement, but most of all, we crave significance—*a sense of purpose.*

When companies connect with their customers' deep emotional motivators, the pay-off can be huge. In the *HBR* article I mentioned earlier, the authors cited the success of a credit card campaign designed to emotionally connect with Millennials. After a well-known bank crafted messages that connected to the emotional desires of the generation, they saw use among the market segment grow by 70 percent.

That's *70*, with a zero after the seven. They didn't change the product. They just changed which emotions buyers connected *to* the product.

The food chain Chipotle Grill created one of the most famous emotion-based ad campaigns in recent history—one that spread to 6.5 million YouTube subscribers in less than two weeks.[3] The ad tugs at our heartstrings by increasing customer awareness of animal confinement, growth hormones, and toxic pesticides. This shows that even a fear of negative and painful emotions drive sales. (This was before their negative press regarding foodborne illnesses in 2015.)

Advertisers drive our purchase decisions by linking high-end kitchen stores with elegance, lingerie with sex, and candles with a feeling of revival. No one is immune. Just last week, I paid double the price for a Smart Water over a generic brand to keep me going during an upcoming business meeting. (I always wonder: If that water's so smart, how come it can't avoid being drunk by someone?)

It makes you wonder: Do we buy anything without emotion? Several years back, I found myself sitting next to the vice president of sales for one of the top tire companies in America. After explaining to him what I did for a living, I said, "I suppose it's a little tough to sell tires emotionally."

"Are you kidding me?" he laughed. "Haven't you seen the baby ads?"

Then I remembered the famous Michelin tire commercials from the 1980s: *"Because so much is riding on your tires!"* I realized that Michelin had bought and paid for—decades earlier—space in my brain that said, "Michelin is the safest tire." Wow!

There's no question that you and I make purchase decisions based on unconscious yearnings and emotional motivators. The question is: What are the most common motivators? What are the drivers that cause us to act, buy, and consume?

For years, my training has centered on highlighting the few core emotional motivators that salespeople must uncover and sell to. New research bears out what I've been saying. With the help of experts and social scientists, the authors of the *HBR* piece created a "standard lexicon of emotions," and in so doing, gave us a list of 300 emotional motivators that contribute to purchasing decisions.

Here are the seven motivators I've found to be particularly powerful:

1. **Safety:** Pick up the newspaper on any day of the week, and you'll see the extent to which humans move toward safety and away from danger. The U.S. Department of Defense spends more than 57 million dollars per *hour* to keep the American people safe. The need for self-protection is a desire that is timeless and universal.

   Our brains are hard-wired for self-preservation. We buy life insurance, make financial investments, vote, and choose mates to secure a comfortable future. We hunger today—and postpone immediate gratification—for a more secure tomorrow.

   Our desire for safety and security is a common motivator for products like:

   * Banking.
   * Real estate.

* Certain types of software.
* Pharmaceuticals and healthcare products and services.

2. **Adventure:** We invest in fly-fishing trips, four-wheel Jeeps, and the latest in fancy gadgets so as to grow, play, and experience new things. We drink unblended Scotch, play cards, travel to Tahiti, dance, ride rollercoasters, and jump out of airplanes (well, some people do) to stimulate our desire for adventure.

   Simple and complex pleasures drive us to do everything from wandering into a cookie store and buying extra chocolate chips to investing in a pontoon boat.

   Our desire for adventure is a common motivator for products like:

* Vacations.
* Automobiles.
* Fashion.
* New technologies.
* Fine wine.
* Beverages.

3. **Significance:** Tony Robbins says it best in his TED Talk, "Why We Do What We Do": "We all need to feel important, special, unique. You can get it by making more money or being more spiritual. You can do it by getting yourself in a situation where you put more tattoos and earrings in places humans don't want to know. Whatever it takes."[4]

   People today are consumed with a desire for "likes," friends, connections, and fame. The average Millennial today shifts between devices like phones and laptops 25 times every non-working hour (and probably even more when they're supposed to be working).

   A few months ago I attended a training session where I heard Oprah Winfrey has probably interviewed more people than anyone else on the planet—from heads of states to rock stars to presidents. Whether the Duchess of York, Tom Cruise, or Michael Jackson, at the end of the show, when the lights go down, these international celebrities all asked Oprah the same question: "How did I do?"

It just shows you that fame doesn't keep people from feeling insecure. In fact, nothing does, because life itself is insecure. A desire to feel that our life is significant is a common motivator for products like:

* Branded accessories.
* Fancy cars.
* Members-only clubs.
* Hotels.
* Home furnishings.
* Athletic wear.

4. **Relationships:** Relationships give meaning to what would otherwise be a lonely, angst-ridden existence. Connection is why we're here; it's how we make it through heartbreak, death, birth, and jealousy. Feelings of disconnection are usually found at the heart of shame and pain. Research shows that people with stronger relationships have tougher immune systems; they get sick less often and heal faster when they do. Research shows that we're happier, more successful, and healthier when we're surrounded by a large social support system.

A desire to connect is a common motivator for products such as:

* Jewelry.
* Food and alcohol.
* Beauty products.
* Coffee houses.
* Travel.

5. **Health and wellness:** Health in today's world means more than just not getting sick. It reflects our deep yearning to feel good and look good. The popularity of spas, revitalizing creams,

supplements, and *you deserve it*-type products and services has increased 50-fold over the past few years. We're tired, overworked, and jam-packed with to-dos. Revitalization products promise a mental, physical, and emotional retreat—and you bet consumers will pay for it!

Connection is a common motivator for products such as:

* Spa services.
* Supplements.
* Weight loss.
* Yoga and meditation classes.
* Health clubs.

6. **Success/sense of purpose:** In *Mr. Holland's Opus*, Richard Dreyfuss plays a professional musician and composer who accepts a job as a high school music teacher in order to spend time with his new wife. Through the span of three decades, Mr. Holland forms close relationships with his students, and mentors hundreds of students in music and in life. When the school decides to close the music department in favor of sports and other academics, he comes to believe that his students have forgotten him, that his life was without purpose. On his final day as a teacher, his wife and son lead him to the school auditorium, where hundreds of his former students, now grown, have gathered to celebrate his retirement and his life's achievements. Overwhelmed with emotion, Mr. Holland finally realizes his masterpiece.[5]

This story makes me cry every time I think of it. It reminds me of the importance of defining our life purpose. Our day-to-day goals are but a smokescreen for the sense of purpose that burns within us. The desire for a sense of purpose is a common motivator for products that:

* Leave a legacy.
* Offer us the opportunity to give back.
* Have investment potential.

7. **Growth and education:** Science confirms that humans naturally search for order and reason; we want explanations for how objects, people, and processes work. However, there are other reasons we seek knowledge. We're curious. We want to pass down what we've learned to the next generation in the hopes that they won't repeat our own foolish choices. But it's more than that. Knowledge makes us more interesting. Smart is sexy! It makes us better able to attract mates, more likely to excel in business, and more likely to contribute to the success of the community, all of which are traits that evolution has bred into us. The impulse toward education is as much a part of our DNA as our eye color.

A need for education and growth is a common motivator for products like:

* Advanced training courses and programs.
* Educational books and videos.
* Coaching and mentoring services.

When you ask anyone over the age of 21, "What's the most important thing in your life?" you'll hear some variations on those seven desires. The order may be different, but our basic needs are universal. Throughout our lives, our core motivators will shift and twist, but in my experience, people find common themes that they return to time and again.

Mistakes That Prevent Us From Discovering Our Customers' Core Motivators

Even the most seasoned salespeople make mistakes that prevent us from truly unearthing our customers' emotional motivators. The following are the most common missteps salespeople make that prevent us from really digging deep.

1. **We offer unimportant, irrelevant information.**

When salespeople don't uncover their customers' core motivators, they risk offering general and irrelevant information. I call this the "shotgun approach": We fire off feature after feature, hoping that one of them will hit its target.

Research suggests that if you give someone too many options, eventually that person will just stop paying attention. Our brains are configured to make a certain number of decisions per day and once we reach that limit—our "saturation point"—we can't make any more, regardless of how important they are. (Former President Obama has been quoted as saying that he makes his most important decisions in the morning while he's still fresh.) Salespeople must keep their presentations simple and on point to keep customers engaged.

2. **We fail to demonstrate actionable value.**

To trigger a buying decision, we need to tailor the value to the customer. Most salespeople fail because they offer $200,000 solutions to $25,000 problems.

For example, Tanya sells executive training programs to Fortune 500 companies. She recently complained to me that she lost a big deal and didn't know why. Her conversation with the prospect went something like this:

Prospect: We're looking for training for our managers.

Tanya: Wonderful. Did you look on our website? What interests you?

Prospect: The emotional intelligence stuff. How much is it?

Tanya: How many people do you want to send?

Prospect: Our 15 department heads.

Tanya: Okay, that will be $5,000 apiece—or $75,000 altogether.

Prospect: Oh, that's way over our budget.

Tanya: What's your budget?

Prospect: About $10,000.

Tanya: Well, you can send two people then.

Prospect: Thank you anyway.

After hearing of Tanya's lost sale, I offered her a bit of coaching.

"Just because a customer calls you and tells you they want to buy a product from you doesn't mean they're *ready* to buy it from you," I told her. "It's easy to uncover customer problems. The hard part is helping them see their problems as painful enough that they're willing to buy now."

I gave Tanya some suggestions for what to do next time she received a similar inquiry.

* Ask questions about why the customer is interested in your programs.
* Uncover the potential cost or other negative implications if they don't move forward.
* Share with them the emotional and/or numerical cost of not moving forward.

I'll go into more detail on this process of uncovering problems in a later chapter. For now, though, as we're talking about emotions and sales, here's how it played out when Tanya did a follow-up call.

Tanya: I'm following up on the conversation we had the other day. I'm just curious: Why were you originally interested in training your team?

Prospect: Well, we've had a bit of infighting between our departments.

Tanya: That's not good. Tell me more.

Prospect: The salespeople don't trust management—and management is blaming sales for the lack of performance. We've had massive turnover. We've lost six managers and 14 salespeople this year.

Tanya: Wow! What does it cost you to recruit a salesperson? The national average is about $40,000.

Prospect: That's about right. And managers cost even more to replace! It's been a mess.

Tanya: Our EQ program has reduced turnover by 50 percent. That program alone could save you over $300,000 next year. You could save your department!

As a result of this call, *25* managers attended the training. Why? Because Tanya followed a sales process, asked deeper questions, and showed the prospect that the financial and emotional value of the purchase far surpassed the price.

3. **We lower the price instead of appealing to core motivators.**

What would it mean to you if you doubled your income—with the same number of customers? Think about how it would feel to give the same amount of effort and earn two, three, or many more times as much.

Last week, I visited a client in Colorado and discovered their top salesperson, Brent, earns more than *five times as much* as the lowest performer in his company while talking to the exact same number of customers. Brent earns more than $500,000 per year and his colleague (at least his colleague *for now*) earns less than $80,000.

What made the difference? Brent creates emotional value rather than haggling about the price. He sticks to his guns when the customer tries to negotiate, and he's never afraid to create tension and let the customer walk away.

If you're not afraid to lose, you'll never win.

Negotiating price can work with small purchases, but can backfire if not done correctly with larger-priced items. Why? When you sell higher-priced items, you're better off increasing the emotional value rather than or at least before lowering your price.

Every time I travel to Mexico, the street vendors try to sell me wool blankets. "Miss, would you like a nice blanket? For you, only 400 pesos. No? How about 300? Special price for today only: 20 pesos!"

In my broken Spanish, I politely tell them price is not the issue. It's 95 degrees and 100 percent humidity. How about a Popsicle?

Now, of course, many tourists simply want an inexpensive reminder of their trip, and the vendors know that. But when price becomes the only differentiator, the path of least resistance is to drop the price, change the offer, or throw in a whole lot of extras. When we sell to core motivators, on the other hand, we link value to emotions, and *when the emotional value is strong enough, the objections go away.*

If those vendors in Puerto Vallarta had only asked the right questions, they might have found out that my Grandpa Joe had given me one of those blankets for my dorm room, but it was lost when I moved. Had they asked if I had ever had such a beautiful blanket or if it was cold where I lived, I just might have bought it for the full 500 pesos.

Salespeople often drop their price out of fear or insecurity, because they think customers expect them to do so, or because *they're* the ones who can't afford what they're selling. You need to be confident in your offer and figure out an emotional value that far exceeds your price.

4. **We sell to secondary motivators instead of linking our offering to our customer's core motivator.**

The average salesperson promotes secondary motivators like saving money or "owning a nicer model." Good salespeople focus on a customer's core emotional motivators, not simply the features that define their product offerings.

If your value proposition centers around saving money, try focusing on the emotional benefits they'll receive from the savings: Tell them what they can *do* with the money they save. My stepson Isaac sells solar panels. He's risen to the top 20 percent in his company. When I asked him how he beats the competition, he replied:

> All the other sales guys talk about the money the customer will save by installing the panels. I spend a bit more time with my customers. I dig deeper.
>
> Last night, I found out that Mrs. O'Neil was intent on refurbishing her kitchen. So, I not only told her she'd save $300 per month, but I recommended

she use part of the monthly savings to finally upgrade her kitchen with marble countertops and top-of-the-line appliances. I even recommended a contractor. She bought on the spot!

5. **We fail to listen.**

Too many salespeople are so busy thinking about what to say next that they never really let what the customer says sink in. They miss opportunities to dig deeper.

"We have all been so busy broadcasting our message," says speaker and sales trainer Linda Clemons, "and we are not tuning in. Thus we don't get the right signal. We don't get the right station. We don't make the connection."[6]

Halfway into my first year in sales, my regional manager, Tom Bennett, shared the story of Bill James, the best salesman he had ever met. James had sold to the last 18 out of 20 customers; there was no stopping him. We all gathered around to learn the details. "What does he say?" we wanted to know. "Where did he get his leads? What does he tell them?"

Tom replied: "He just listens so hard it hurts."

Better Than Big Data

Today, companies invest in big data and analytics in the hopes of learning about their customer's emotional motivators.

Although most salespeople don't have access to a multimillion-dollar advertising budget, you do have access to something much more powerful. You are face-to-face or on the phone with your customer. You have the ability to create trust, build rapport, ask questions, and tailor your presentation to your customer perfectly.

Think for a moment about what's at the core—the very core—of what you're promoting right now: What emotional need will it satisfy?

If you think deeply about your product or service in this way you will rise above the competition.

PUT IT INTO ACTION

Don't Forget What Motivates *You*

It's important to know why your customers make buying decisions, but there's another very important part of the equation: understanding why you're selling. Only when you know why you're working hard will you keep on working when the going gets tough. Ask yourself:

* What motivates you to make a change instead of remaining comfortable and secure?
* What drives you to do what you do every day?
* If no one were watching, would you do what you do anyway? Why or why not?
* What keeps you from picking up the phone, making the calls, and hearing the "no's"? Is it a child, a dream, a lover?

Answering these questions will bring you one step closer to selling with heart. You don't need to share these responses with me, your spouse, or anyone else, for that matter. No one's looking. You're the only one who can know what drives you. Knowing your own reasons for doing the work you do—whatever they are—puts you in touch with the same emotional motivators that drive your customers. So give it your all. Answer from your gut. Know yourself.

CHAPTER 3

Freedom Lives in Structure

Universal Truth #3: Pilots run through preflight checklists. Free-throw shooters develop rituals to help them hit the same shot time and again. Bakers adhere to time-tested recipes. So why should it be different in sales? Highly successful salespeople have a process they follow, and they follow that process every time. It may sound counterintuitive, but structure creates the freedom to act authentically and to create true connection.

Create a Recipe for Success

A few months ago, I met a mortgage saleswoman named Kendra. I liked her immediately. She has enthusiasm and innate talent—plus she taught me how to use Instagram.

Three years ago, she was the top seller at her company. "Going to work every day was such a high," she said. "I was on top of the world!"

And suddenly everything changed.

"I couldn't maintain my balance," she said. "I was working so hard. The long hours and the intensity sent me into a downward spiral."

Frustrated, Kendra became overwhelmed with all the reasons her prospects didn't want to buy. The economy had taken a dive, her leads were stale, her company's rates weren't competitive enough—you name it. Seeking greener pastures, she accepted an offer from a competitor, and then another, until she eventually left the mortgage business altogether.

After she told me all this, I asked Kendra to recite her presentation. It was impressive. Creating a connection with prospects, finding out what mattered most to them, and overcoming objections seemed to come easily to her.

But when I asked her *why* she was saying what she did, she couldn't articulate an answer.

"It just seemed right to say those things," she said.

Like many salespeople, Kendra had never put her presentation down in writing. She had never defined the steps to her sales process. She had never stopped to think about *why* her prospects bought or *why* they didn't. In other words, she didn't have a recipe for success. She never knew if she left out a key ingredient, or if she'd added in another that she didn't need.

Because she lacked a process, she lacked consistency. Because she lacked consistency, she lacked confidence. Because she lacked confidence, her work and her life felt out of control.

Sound familiar?

I've met hundreds of salespeople and sales leaders just like Kendra. Lack of a process is a common obstacle to sales mastery.

As a sales professional, you need a process. It keeps you on track, freeing you up to listen and connect with your prospects. If you manage a team, or hope to one day, you need to know what you're doing right so you can repeat your process, scale it, and teach it to others. The good news is that although a lack of process is a common problem, it's one that's easily solved.

Systematize Basic "Must-Do's"

All professionals need some form of structure in order to do their jobs well. Without processes, planes would collide in the air, basketball players would loft air balls instead of making foul shots, and surgeons would allow their emotions and impulses to derail them in the operating room.

So why should it be any different in sales? Good salespeople know their sales steps; they have structures, systems, and rituals. The best salespeople understand the psychology behind the steps so that if they go off track or fall into a slump, they can pull themselves out of it. Fast.

This may all sound boring. You might say, "Yuck, how monotonous! I got into sales so I could have more freedom than my friends in finance. I need spontaneity, not rigidity."

First of all, you can be a lot more spontaneous in every aspect of your life when you're bringing home the Benjamins. Trust me.

But you might be wondering what structure has to do with selling with heart.

Don't confuse structure with rigidity or a lack of sincerity. Ironically, systematizing the basic "must-do's" of our presentations is what gives us freedom to be spontaneous, fun, and authentic.

Fly the Plane

If I didn't structure my time to write this book for seven hours each day, I'd never have written it. I'd have made excuses: "I don't feel creative today; Susan wants to go on a hike; I work better under pressure." Or as the saying goes, "The sooner you fall behind, the more time you have to catch up."

Structure saves us from having to ask questions like: Should I prospect this morning? Should I skip the rapport-building step because my prospect is in a hurry? Which discovery questions do I ask? Having a structure means you stop asking whether or not you feel like doing your job today. You just do it.

Here's the cool part: when you follow a basic roadmap, eventually it becomes second nature. Have you ever heard someone say of a fellow salesperson, "Oh, he's a natural!"? There's no such thing. He just practiced so hard that his skills seem innate. The people who rise to the top understand this.

Without structure, salespeople fall victim to their emotions, external dramas, and whims. You're tired from a big night out, so you say, "I'll skip that warm-up step just this once." Danger! My husband's a pilot. He has a saying: "Fly the plane." In other words, keep an eye on what's in front of you. You need to make a checklist, fly the plane, and know when to compensate for turbulence, so you can land the deal smoothly.

Yes, it takes time and commitment to come up with a structure that works for you, but rigorous focus, planning, and repetition ensures that you won't skip a step of your presentation, perform it haphazardly, or simply wing it.

You need to know your product, your steps, and your methods backward and forward so that the mechanics become effortless and your passion becomes contagious. Only when the basics of your presentation are familiar can you forget about them.

As Eric Greitans writes in *Resilience*, "In ancient Greece, repetition was an unexpected and integral part of philosophy. The Greeks understood that shaping human behavior requires repetition. We can lose focus, we take a day off and then we forget what inspired us in the first place and to prevent these things from happening, the slackening of effort that can come in any practice, we build structures of repetition into our lives."[1]

Process frees your mind so you can open your heart to the person in front of you.

Typically, people fall into one of three categories when it comes to sales processes:

1. **They simply don't have a process.**

   You've already heard about how Kendra's lack of structure tanked her sales. Some salespeople claim they can manage without a structure. Maybe they can for a stretch, but they inevitably hit a wall where they just can't figure out what's working and what isn't.

   A lack of structure is even more dangerous when you're a sales manager. Last night, I was speaking with a friend who runs a large nonprofit. Twelve salespeople report to Jenny, but she herself lands double the donations of all her employees combined. Sounds like something's off, doesn't it?

When I asked her about her sales process, she was stumped. Jenny knew exactly what to do, but she had never defined a structure to share with her team. When you sell on personality and instinct alone, you can't teach others or increase your own effectiveness.

2. **They have a process, but they don't understand the psychology behind their process.**

You must not only define the steps of your sales process, you must learn the psychology, skills, and tools needed to perform each step effectively.

When I was little girl, I used to love to play games more than anything else in the world. Monopoly, Risk, Clue, you name it! It became a family joke. Whenever I explained to others how to play, I would declare, "The object of the game is to win." That was it. No rules, no strategies, no nothing—just win!

Too many salespeople enter the sales game thinking the same thing. Although you're partly right, each step of your process has a unique goal, specific strategies, and must-do's that, if performed correctly, will ultimately win you the sale. Sales psychology not only involves knowing what and how to perform each step, it means knowing *why* you're performing each step. Knowing the "why behind the what" helps you adapt.

Look, when you're selling, stuff happens. You forget your materials, the model isn't available, or the technology is jammed. Savvy salespeople understand that a bit of structure combined with psychological insight gives them the ability to react creatively and authentically in response to changes or disruptions.

If you believe in sticking to exact scripts, you probably believe in the tooth fairy.

Scripts are fine so long as the prospect sticks to their script. The problem is that they never do! Recently, I listened to an inside sales rep ask a prospect how her day was going.

The response: "Horrible. My schnauzer died last night."

The rep's response: "That's great. We have good weather here, too."

(I couldn't make this stuff up.)

Had the rep simply been taught that the most important goal early in the call is to build rapport, she may have shown a little empathy for the poor schnauzer.

3. **They have a process—but they don't stick to it.**

Just as you need to stick to your workout if you want results, you need to continually monitor your process and solicit feedback from a mentor or colleague to make sure you're maximizing your effectiveness.

You can use other tools, as well. Ongoing training and checklists are two of the best ways to stay on track so you don't skip steps and lose deals.

In his book *The Checklist Manifesto,* Atul Gawande tells a story of the U.S. Army's flight competition for airplane manufacturers vying to build the next-generation long-range bomber.[2] The truth is that the competition was more of a formality because Boeing's Model 299 could carry more bombs and fly faster and almost twice as far.

Yet, as impressive as it was, the first Model 299 crashed into a fiery explosion right on the runway. An investigation revealed a pilot error. The Boeing model was deemed too complicated for one man to fly.

The Army decided to purchase a couple of Boeings as test planes anyway and came up with an ingeniously simple approach: Rather than making the Model 299 pilots go through more training, they created *pilot's checklists*. What was the result? With the checklist in the pilot's hand, the Model 299, which became the B-17 bomber, took a total of 1.8 million flights without an accident!

I recommend creating your own checklist. Write down the steps of your sales process. Tailor it to your product with any additional methods or rituals that need to be added. For example, you might want to customize your list with reminders such as: send a brochure, follow up with an e-mail, or show the model.

On the following page, you'll find an example of a sales presentation evaluation we created for a client. Managers use it to shadow salespeople and offer constructive feedback. This checklist helps keep salespeople on track.

Keep in mind that there's no one right sales process. Depending on your organization, you might already have a basic process or sales steps you've been encouraged to follow. What I'm suggesting is that you have some basic plan so that if things go off course, you can adapt. "What sets successful organizations apart isn't the type of sales methodology they use," says Glenn Seninger, group vice president at Oracle. "It's the rigor in which they follow their process, whatever that process might be. A commitment to consistency delineates winning cultures."[3]

Lay the Groundwork

If you're still trying to figure out the steps of your process, here are some basic guidelines:

1. **Number your steps.**

   A few months ago, my team was working with a communications company based outside of Toronto. Not only were their individual sales steps in a different order, each salesperson had a different number of steps. Some had 12 steps, some of the veterans had 17, and the new training manager, Greta, insisted on 36! No wonder one of the biggest complaints of sales leaders is a lack of consistency.

Pts	Step	Sales Presentation Evaluation (100 Points Total)				
5	Pre-Presentation Preparation	Get in peak state (1)	No Prejudging (1)	Visualize Result (1)	Arrive 5 minutes early (1)	Get Centered (1)
5	Meet and Greet	First impression (1)	Hospitality (1)	Professionalism (1)	Friendly Smile and Handshake (1)	Transfer Enthusiasm (1)
10	Warm-Up	Rapport questions (5)	Ask About THEM (3)	Credibility Statement (2)		
5	Agenda	Expectations for Today—Agenda, Setup Discovery (3)		Easy Transition (2)		
10	Company Story	Clarity (2)	Timeline (2)	Awards (2)	Expansion (2)	Stay on Track (2)
20	Discovery	Identifying Problems (5)	Uncovering Objections (5)	Establishing Product Positioning (5)		Uncover DBM (5)
5	Discovery Confirmation	DBM (2)	Problem (2)	Possible Objection (1)		
15	Product Positioning / Presentation	Questions of use (3)	Ease of communicating points (3)	Third Party stories (3)	Linking, Discovery Information (6)	
5	Pricing	Business Case (1)	Sell the QUALITY (2)	Emphasize BENEFITS (1)	Put them in the Picture (1)	
10	Summary and Closing	Summarize Entire Presentation (2)	Bring Value Proposition Back (2)	Ask for the Business (2)	Isolate Objections (real) (2)	Overcome Objections (2)
	Additional Points	Timing and Flow of Presentation				
		Overcoming Objections				
				Total Points		
	Areas of Excellence	1.				
		2.				
	Areas For Improvement	1.				
		2.				

It doesn't matter how many steps there are in your process (though—with all due respect to Greta—36 means start trimming the fat!). Here's what does matter: Identify steps that are repeatable and have proven to be effective. Make sure they follow a logical order (more about that later in the chapter).

2. **Name your steps.**

You need to name the individual steps of your presentation. This will help you remember which stage of the process you're in and will help you strategize the next steps. Don't get too clever with names. A recent client called their presentation step "The Octopus" because it had eight parts. Confusing!

3. **Adopt the "no matter what rule."**

Years ago, a large hospitality company hired my team to build a comprehensive training program for more than 100 of their sales sites. Our first action was to study the top performers and craft a system to scale effective behaviors. The executives directed us to one of their top directors, Maria Margenot. Maria's team was out-producing any other team in the company. After meeting her, it was easy to see why. It wasn't just that she's clever and a lifelong learner, it's that she masterminded a system she referred to as "non-negotiables." Maria maintains non-negotiables are part of her team's "no matter what rule." Without non-negotiables, you'll forget important steps and omit best practices.

Says Maria: "Non-negotiables are foundational must-do's that contribute to the sale and the prospect experience. We designated very few, so everybody can know and memorize them. I believe that when you have non-negotiables, or core principles, it actually frees you because knowing your basic structure, you can focus on bringing your authentic, creative personality and self to work each day."

What are your non-negotiables? They will differ company to company and, unless mandated, from salesperson to salesperson. Here are some ideas to get you started:

* Always be prepared to meet your prospects five minutes early.
* Ask a specific set of discovery questions to ensure you uncover their emotional needs and pain points.
* Polish your shoes.
* Return client calls or e-mails within 24 hours.
* Always show the promotional film.
* Make sure you tell at least three evocative stories.

"Non-negotiables make salespeople feel safe," says Maria, "but, more importantly, they allow them to be their authentic selves."[4]

4. **Develop technical prowess.**

Maria is also a huge advocate of developing your technical prowess. You can't be fussing with your online demo, losing your passwords, or tampering with any other technical aspects of your presentation and create an authentic connection. Unless you get the technical stuff down pat, you'll be fretting about synching your technology rather than synching with your prospect.

Sting is one of my all-time favorite artists. When he plays "Wrapped Around Your Finger," I can feel his heart and soul. I'm sure he has bucket loads of technical knowledge, but the fact that he's mastered his craft allows him to express the spirit in his music. In sales, you have to take your sales prowess to the level where you can focus on the prospect, not your instruments.

5. **Remember the buying process.**

One of my favorite exercises at workshops involves asking participants, usually salespeople and sales leaders, to write down the steps of their sales process. Most of them jot down the individual steps they perform with ease. What always strikes me is how frequently salespeople who work in the exact same organizations—salespeople who've had the exact same training—come up with completely different results. It's dramatic!

After that, I ask a simple question: What are the steps of the buying process? Not the sales process; the *buying* process.

The nervous laughter is profound. Participants giggle, shuffle in their seats, and ultimately start whispering among themselves. That's when I hammer home the point:

We spend far too much time talking about the sales process, but not nearly enough time understanding the buying process.

Remember: Buyers' decisions are driven by their emotional brain. Do you ever look at a prospect and ask yourself, "What is going on in their brain right now?" I'm glad you asked. It may be the most important question you can ask yourself while selling and it's critical to creating structure.

In the early 1960s, Paul MacLean was credited with modeling the triune theory of the brain.[5] According to this research, there are three parts to the human brain. (Recently, neuroscientists are debating the validity of the triune concept, but I can tell you firsthand, I've been teaching it for more than 15 years, and salespeople report this psychological understanding of human behavior has done more to augment their success than any other lesson in human psychology. So let's go with it!)

Here's why the revelation is important to us: Your prospect is in one of those three parts of the brain at every moment of the sales conversation. Your job is to recognize exactly where she is at any given moment and act accordingly.

Without getting overly technical, MacLean called the first part of the brain the "reptilian brain."

Think of your prospect as transforming himself or herself into an iguana. Ever seen an iguana? They're kind of creepy. All they think about is survival.

When your prospect is in reptilian brain mode, all she's thinking about is problems and money—specifically, that it's a huge problem that you want so much money for whatever you're selling. She's not thinking about how much she really wants the thing you're selling. She's just staring at you like a beady-eyed iguana, not even blinking, just wanting to crawl under a rock somewhere and eat some flies.

It's really tough to make people fall in love with your product when they are in iguana mode.

So your job is to shift them from their reptilian brain to what's called the midbrain. (I didn't make these names up for the parts of the brain, so don't blame me for them.) The easiest way to think of the midbrain is it's your brain on champagne. You've got your party hat on. Basically, the only sound you can hear in the midbrain is "Woo-hoo!" *This* is where you want your prospect. In midbrain mode, they love the world, they love your product, they love you, and they love the idea of whipping out their credit card and buying *right this second*. So if the reptilian brain is symbolized by the gimlet-eyed iguana, the midbrain is the prospect with a party hat on. She's not just sipping, but gulping champagne behind the velvet rope in the VIP section of the hottest club in Vegas at two minutes before midnight.

Ever seen a party hat on an iguana? Nope. It slides right off. That's because you cannot be in two parts of your brain at once. You can be in the iguana, or you can be in the VIP section of the hottest club in Vegas. *But you cannot be in both at the same time.*

Did I mention that there were three parts of the human brain? Right you are. Here's the third part: the neocortex.

In the neocortex, you're being logical and rational. Is this good for me? Is it a good value? Is it safe? Is it long-lasting? Your prospect needs this information, which she will access through the neocortex in order to justify the purchase to her midbrain (and her husband, or anyone else involved in the buying decision).

So your real job is to move the prospect out of iguana mode, get them happy and maybe a little tipsy in the Vegas club, and then bring them into thinking brain, or the neocortex, where you can give them all the logical reasons to justify the purchase that, on an emotional level, they really, really want to make.

Most salespeople make the horrendous mistake of trying to sell features, benefits, logic, and rationality . . . to iguanas. Iguanas couldn't care less about features and benefits. All iguanas want to do is survive, and survival probably means not buying your product because it costs too much money. So, to repeat, you've got to get them out of iguana brain, into the Vegas club, and then into what we could call "calculator phase," where they just need to input the data about how great, efficient, fun, hard-working, long-lasting, and so forth your offering really is.

The next time you're looking at your prospect and wondering, "What exactly is going on in her brain?" now you know. Are they in iguana-land? Are they at the Vegas club? Or are they in calculator mode? Recognize where they are, and move them to where you want them to go.

Putting It All Together: The Critical Steps of a Winning Sales Presentation

Now that you understand the basic building blocks of any presentation, here is a more detailed look at the ingredients of a winning sales process. Again, there is no right method. But you must have definable steps in your sales process that takes into account the iguana and the psychology of the buying process.

1. **Get into peak state.**

   We can't possibly shift our prospect's emotional brain state if we can't identify and manage our own. Getting in your own "peak state"—as my colleague Sean Harrison calls it—takes commitment. Most top performers practice rituals to manage their emotions. I know someone who listens to Aerosmith before each sales call; some pray. You may just take two deep breaths. Do whatever you need to do to prepare your mind because emotions are contagious.

2. **Prepare to prospect.**

   If you're in the business of securing your own leads, this may very well be your most important step. No prospects equals no sales. I was fortunate enough to teach a class with bestselling author, Jill Konrath. One of Jill's great pieces of advice when it comes to prospecting for new accounts is:

   "Frazzled prospects don't want to hear about your products or services. They will grant you access only if you pique their curiosity or provoke their thinking with relevant information such as:

   * How other companies addressed similar issues.
   * Business outcomes they're likely to achieve.
   * Information on industry and competitive trends."[6]

   Your messages must be short, concise, and to the point. Allow time in your day to craft messages that are specific and will resonate with your prospect. Prospect first thing each morning. Well, you may want to grab a cup of coffee and feed the dog first—but after that. Set appointments before you check your e-mail, craft a proposal, or count your commission check. Why? Default mode causes resistance to prospecting. Unless you set aside time each day, a more appealing task, or an offer to meet the iguana at a Vegas club will steal your attention.

3. **The warm-up.**

   The warm-up is simply about building a foundation of trust with the buyer by establishing rapport and demonstrating empathy. (I'll spend a lot of time on this topic in Chapter 5.) Keep in mind that the warm-up is not the same thing as your discovery. Sometimes when salespeople fall into a slump, they interrogate their prospects with discovery questions. This raises the tension and throws your prospect into fear mode. In a warm-up, our goal is to make friends with the iguana—not qualify them! Besides, how can you successfully answer questions before you've discovered what is important to the prospect? The goal here is to move the prospect into party hat mode.

4. **Statement of intent.**

   Early on, make sure to give the prospect an idea of what the sales process is going to look like and what your intentions are. Give them an agenda and discuss expectations. This not only reduces tension, it shows your competency and reliability. Intent statements might begin with, "Here's what you can expect in the process. Many of our prospects have questions about XYZ, so I'm going to begin by answering them for you."

   Without this important step, people can feel manipulated. Here's a perfect example. Years ago, I was on a committee with a woman named Nellie. Fifteen years later, I got a call from Birmingham. Nellie reintroduced herself, and then launched right into trying to build a relationship. After she'd gone on and on, she finally gave me her reason for calling: Her business was failing and she wanted to borrow $10,000! Um, no way!

Iguana alert! Why didn't you tell me your real intention at the beginning?

We can prevent prospects from feeling manipulated or blindsided by being up-front about our intentions right from the start. For example, if you're inviting a friend to lunch to share a business opportunity or to tell them about your financial planning services, make it clear from the beginning that you wish to discuss business, not baseball. We will discuss the intent statement in greater detail in the chapter on trust.

5. **Discovery.**

I also like to call this, "Find out WIFT" (what's in it for them). Salespeople are notorious for pitching products too soon. Buyers decide why they'll buy, not salespeople. By asking "who, what, when, where, why" questions, you will discover facts, feelings, and pain points. In my experience, there's no greater way to increase your efficiency than by asking *great* discovery questions. That's why I've devoted an entire chapter to questions.

6. **Information confirmation (confirm discovery information).**

Once you've uncovered WIFT, repeat back the prospect's core motivators, problems, and objections and—most importantly—gain agreement. (I'll discuss this more deeply in Chapter 8.) Most salespeople don't perform this step. But it's crucial. It allows prospects to, as author Mark Goulston says, "feel felt."[7] It also lets you know that you've heard all the information correctly and helps the prospect understand how your product will solve their specific issues. In longer sales cycles, you should begin every meeting with confirmation about what was discussed in the last meeting.

7. **The product presentation.**

In this step you're performing a demo, showing the model, or somehow demonstrating the experience of using your product. Once you know what's in it for your prospect, explain how your solution will give her more of what she wants and how it will solve her specific problems. Most importantly, you need to change the emotional state of the prospect, and build urgency and excitement so she is receptive to your offer.

8. **Close (or send a proposal).**

It's critical that this last step is clearly defined. The last thing you want to do is give an Olympic-caliber presentation only to fumble at the finish line. Before you ask for the money, send a proposal, or take steps to close, you should solicit feedback. Put the prospect back in control. What do you like about what you've seen so far? How would you use it? Who would use it? Don't ever send a proposal until you've clearly gone over the terms, details, and specifics of your agreement. We will discuss how to isolate objections and ask for the order in Chapter 9.

It's not enough to just add these steps into your sales process. You also need to ask, "*Why* am I doing these steps and how do I go about doing them?" Don't worry if you don't have complete answers yet. That's what this book will help you understand.

Balance Rapport and Urgency

Think about your last few prospect calls. When you first met, were they excited, glad to speak with you, thrilled to buy, or were they suspicious, frazzled, and impatient? If you said the former, I want your job. The truth is that most prospects don't want to be sold to; it's your job to move them from a negative emotional state to a positive one.

Having a structure in place not only helps us increase our consistency, it also keeps us balanced. Take one of the most difficult aspects of selling: the challenge of maintaining true rapport while also creating urgency. How do you connect at a heart level and then role up your sleeves and sell? Most sales leaders have told me their number-one challenge is maintaining the proper tension between the two.

Conventional wisdom has long held that selling is about building rapport and making a friend. Salespeople who were nice, were accommodating, and who sold to a prospect's emotional motivators, made sales and made money.

But customers have changed. They have options and lots of them. With increased choice comes increased complexity. With increased complexity comes analysis paralysis.

There is growing evidence that the best salespeople today are not only skillful at establishing trust, but are respectfully assertive.

According to Mathew Dixon and Brent Adamson in their book, *The Challenger Sale,* sometimes a prospect's greatest need is to figure out what they need.[8] Your role is to help them do that. And doing that takes courage. Your ability to lead with heart, yet also ask the tough questions, will determine your sales success. The best salespeople today balance relationship-building with respectful assertiveness—heart and sell.

In short, top-performing sales reps not only build a structure to ensure they're performing the right steps in the right order, they also know when to turn the heat up or down depending on the emotional reaction of their prospects. In my experience, too many salespeople either lead too accommodating or too aggressive. They don't have the structure, the mastery, or the confidence to make it, as Goldilocks says, *just right.*

Are You Overly Accommodating?

Meet Suzy, the approval seeker.

Suzy gets energized when she greets a new prospect. So much so that people wonder, "How can she be that excited about meeting her 30th prospect this month?"

Suzy agrees with everyone and spends hours with prospects whether they qualify or not. Prospects invite her to their homes for Thanksgiving dinner and even offer to play matchmaker.

Suzy makes friends, but she rarely closes a sale. She is accommodating to a fault.

Do you get the picture? Here are some signs that you, like Suzy, are a bit of a doormat with prospects:

* You create strong relationships, but when it comes time to close the sale, you cower. (You're afraid of offending them or worried it will ruin the relationship, but the whole point of the relationship is that you sell and they buy!)
* You keep hammering the same tired leads instead of focusing on the next prospect.
* You offer extras at the expense of your own commission.
* When you quote price, you're quick to drop it or throw in the trip to Africa, the five-year service deal, or the upgraded sound system. This costs you credibility and respect.

Or Are You Too Aggressive?

Now, meet Tony, the glad hander.

Tony has been around for a while. He speaks quickly, trusts no one, and uses expressions like "Always be closing," "Keep it simple, stupid," "Coffee is for closers," and, of course, "Buyers are liars."

He's memorized a dozen closes and has an answer for everything. He knows the first "no" is just a signal that the game has begun. Tony comes on too strong, just like his aftershave. He doesn't listen and, worst of all, he doesn't sell.

Perhaps you, too, have fallen back on some classic Tony strategies, especially during moments when you feel the prospect pulling away.

How do you know when you're acting like Tony?

* If you sense prospects are losing interest, you start going on and on about the features and benefits of a product without even asking why they would be interested.
* In your misguided attempts to create urgency, you fire off sharp-angle closing techniques.

* When you lose a sale, you invent a lot of excuses for why prospects won't buy, but you never take a critical look at what you may have done wrong.
* You no longer like your job—or your life. You're exhausted, agitated, and overworked. And, of course, none of it is your fault.

You may know a Suzy and a Tony or two, because the sales world is rife with them.

You might also bounce back and forth between the two extremes. When the pressure is on to meet quota, we may turn up the Tony and when we're feeling insecure, we find ourselves struck with a serious case of Suzy syndrome. The good news is that you can structure into your presentation strategies for maintaining a healthy balance between the two poles of accommodation and manipulation. Let's see how the pros do just that.

The Middle Way: Respectfully Assertive

Respectfully assertive salespeople continually ask themselves:

* Am I providing valuable insights that are distinct from my competitors?
* Is my prospect bored?
* Is she engaged?
* Do I need to ask tougher questions?
* Is it time to assume the sale, or is there something else I can assist her with?
* Is she fearful? Have fight-or-flight hormones hijacked her brain? (Is she an iguana right now?)
* Is my prospect becoming nervous?
* Should I ask them to buy now after that obvious buying signal?
* Should I back off?

One of my colleagues, Joe McGriff, used to say the most important job of a salesperson is to manage the emotional state of the client. So if the prospect seems scared, tell a story or ask a question that will help them relive a positive memory. If your prospect seems bored, speed things up, simplify, or use phrases that better align with their values and concerns.

Think less about what you want to say and more about how you want the prospect to feel.

Repetition Is the Key to Success

I remember when I became a new manager; I got to work preparing weekly sales training meetings for my team. I asked my mentor, "After I'm done training the 12 steps of the sales presentation, what shall I train on next?"

His reply: "Start over."

That's so Zen, and so true.

CHAPTER 4

In Sales, No Never Means No

Universal Truth #4: Are you paralyzed by fear? Good. Top salespeople know that the more fear they feel, the more important it is to tackle the fear. What you're afraid to do, you must do. The question you're afraid to ask, you must ask. In this chapter, we'll look at "getting out on the skinny branches." Failure is inevitable. Resilience is a life skill, one that will fill your soul and your pocket.

No Soliciting

My friend John Liner sold encyclopedias door to door in college. Anyone who has ever done this type of sales knows how demoralizing it can be. Most people shoo you away the moment they see you coming.

But John had a mentor who told him something he never forgot. "Go to the houses with the signs that say, 'No soliciting.' They're your best customers."

John was baffled. "How can that be?" he asked. "Clearly they're not interested in buying. That's why they have a sign."

"Quite the opposite," said his mentor. "They're so scared they're going to buy that they put up signs so they can avoid the temptation."

Back in those days, many women were stay-at-home housewives. Their husbands, concerned that their wives would buy anything, insisted that they place a sign in the front window to ward off unwanted salesmen.

John took the advice to heart. He targeted those homes with the signs and sold to nearly every one of them. He became the top salesman in his region.

The story gets better. As a young entrepreneur, John got an idea. Instead of selling encyclopedias, he'd sell "No soliciting" signs to those households that didn't have them. When someone would answer the door, John would say, "I bet you're sick and tired of getting bothered by door-to-door salesmen like me. Buy my sign and it will ward off all of those obnoxious salesmen behind me."

John paid his way through college and then some!

Target the "No's"

Too many salespeople panic at the thought of hearing "no." I understand why. If you're like most people, your earliest memories from childhood sounded like, "No! You can't have the cookie. . . . No! You can't go outside now. . . ." From an early age, we learn to recoil at the very word.

In sales though, as in life, if you never deal with your resistance to the word "no," you will never reach your goals.

Salespeople are often taught that no's are a necessary evil, or a hurdle to overcome. But top performers think of no's differently. They look for the no's. Instead of setting goals for the number of yeses they get, they actually celebrate their no's and learn from them.

Not only was my encyclopedia-selling friend John not afraid of the word no, he specifically targeted the no's.

Once you understand why you need the no's, you will uncover objections, make the tough calls, and find creative ways to break through walls and barriers. Nice guys don't finish last—quitters do. Ask an Olympian.

Get Out on the Skinny Branches

Go after the low-hanging fruit and you'll be competing against lots of cherry-pickers. Take the more difficult path and you will reap greater rewards. Or as my friend, a sales manager, puts it: "Get out on the skinny branches."

He likens sales success to climbing out on the skinny branches of a tree. "The most important sales virtue is courage," he says. Top performers take chances. They create strategies to face rejection, and they accept that failure is an inevitable and necessary stop on the road to success.

Summon Your Courage to Face Your Fears

* The call you're afraid to make is the call you must make.
* The question you're afraid to ask is the question you must ask.
* The conversation you're most afraid to have is the one you must have.

Try it. Right now. Make a list of the 10 people that you are most afraid or embarrassed to contact: the big accounts, the ones you're not ready to call, the scary ones. Great! That's the easy part. The hard, but most satisfying part comes next. Pick up the phone, knock on the door, reach out to those people, and go for the sale!

Let "No" Fuel You

Think for a moment about our heroes, entrepreneurs, and thought leaders, and their accomplishments. I guarantee they've all made their mark in the face of massive opposition.

* J.K. Rowling was rejected by dozens of publishers, including Penguin, before the *Harry Potter* series was picked up by a small London publishing house—all because her 8-year-old daughter persisted and insisted that Rowling continue to submit her manuscript.[1]

* Decca Recording told the Beatles, "We don't like your sound, and guitar music is on the way out."[2]
* In *Black's Law Dictionary*, 3rd edition (published prior to 1969), the definition of commercial impossibility is "a trip to the moon."

Are you chasing the larger deals or settling for the easier targets? Do you look for the good in failure, or do you play the victim and blame external circumstances? The bottom line is that you must accept the fact that you'll never become a powerful sales pro without sometimes coming off as a complete joke and embarrassment. It comes with the territory.

Once you change your mindset regarding the word "no," you'll change your sales and your life. But, as I'll discuss in the pages that follow, change takes courage. Courage is the virtue that enables people to move through rejection and become stronger. No one will ever escape pain, suffering, and failure. Yet from pain can come courage; from courage, comes strength.

Why You Need "No"

1. **No makes you stronger.**

   If you had never experienced failure, would you be who you are today? Really? I've interviewed thousands of sales leaders through the years and one thing many share is this: When I asked them, "If you had one 'do-over,' what would it be?" they almost all said something like, "Nothing. My mistakes have gotten me to where I am today."

   Of course, when they're fresh, mistakes hurt. But if you look back during your life, my guess is it's the times when you've changed careers, lost your partner, or endured some other hardship that you really grew. You emerged from these setbacks stronger—with new skills and experiences. Here are my toughest moments and why I'm glad they happened:

* Had I not undergone a dreadful divorce, I wouldn't have gained the knowledge I needed to build a relationship with my true love.

* Had I not ended a business relationship poorly, I wouldn't have learned how to better resolve conflict.

* Had I not been fired from my job in my early 30s, I wouldn't have pursued my dream and started a training company. I'll never forget the crushing anguish I felt after hearing the words: "We did all we could. We're so sorry." Driving away from the Denver Marriott, I switched on the radio. Playing was an Eagles song with the lyrics: *In a New York minute, anything can change.* Suddenly, tears were streaming down my face. One year later, I knew this was the best thing that could have happened to me.

Being in sales definitely has an emotional cost, but it has even more rewards. I've never wondered if I chose the right profession or if it was worth it. The ability to help others, to lead, and to learn from my failures has hurt like hell, but I have always felt human and alive. Failure is always less painful when you extract value from it and share lessons learned with others. Look at failure as an opportunity to test your default modes: Are they helping or hindering your growth and your productivity?

2. **No makes you fearless.**

We all have fears. And the fear of rejection often tops the list. This fear holds some people back from prospecting; even picking up the phone can be terrifying.

I find that when I distinguish exactly what my fears are and ask myself, "What's the worst thing that can happen?" I feel less scared. The truth is, the worst thing is typically that I may feel embarrassed or unworthy, and that's not as bad as not going for what I want.

When you're feeling afraid, take a chance; be bold and tell a friend or mentor exactly what your biggest fears are. Here are mine (these don't include my personal fears like losing my family, getting old, and living in an apartment with a poodle in the Fairfax district):

* I'll never be as good as (fill in the blanks: my mother, my brother, my colleagues, my competitors).
* I really don't know what I'm doing. I'm in over my head.
* I won't have anything new to say.
* I'm a has-been.
* People will laugh at me.
* My life won't make a difference.

Ughhhhh. That was hard. But I feel better now and so will you if you try it. Take a moment and write down your biggest fears. What's the worst thing that could happen if . . . ?

Your fears may be holding you back. Writing them down will help you to move through them, and sharing them will help you realize that most big fears are universal. Many of us, for example, fear our emotions. But as we will see, good salesmanship requires empathy. In other words, we must be able to read, understand, and actually feel another person's emotions. Sometimes that "feeling" part is really uncomfortable. So we avoid it. But when we do, we kill our chances of uncovering a customer's problem and delivering the right solution.

As we'll discuss in greater detail in Chapter 9, there's a big difference between empathetic "emotional selling" and "selling emotionally"—succumbing to our own negative emotions and tendencies. Sales leader and author of *Emotional Intelligence for Salespeople* Colleen Stanley has said that one of the biggest challenges for salespeople is overcoming our fight-or-flight reactions: when we're experiencing fear, we become self-focused and self-centered, more worried about what's going on inside ourselves than what's going on with the prospect or client.[3] When something your prospect says triggers you, Stanley suggests trying to name the emotion you're feeling. Feeling frustrated is very different than feeling humiliated. They require different solutions.

Stop taking "no's" personally and your embarrassment and shame will start to disappear. After all, haven't you said no to someone you like and admire? Sometimes the timing was wrong. Sometimes the offer wasn't right. You had to say no. If you can say it, you can hear it.

3. **No makes you money.**

Have you ever landed a sale with no objections? I mean, not one "no" or even an "I'm uncomfortable with this or that"? That's not selling; that's just taking an order. You might as well ask, "Do you want fries with that?" Objections are a critical part of your sales process. Objections mean your customer is interested. Hooray!

If they weren't interested, they wouldn't put out the energy. I remember one time I attended a personal growth seminar in Oahu. One of the girls, Kim, was desperately trying to get over a recent breakup. One morning, I noticed Kim lacing up her running shoes. "Where are you going?" I asked.

"I'm jogging to the other side of the island to find my ex-boyfriend. I can't wait to tell him 'I'm over you. I finally don't love you anymore!'"

"So let me get this right," I said. "You're going to jog 12 miles to Diamond Head and then—dripping with sweat, panting from a lack of breath—you will face your boyfriend and tell him you no longer care? That you've moved on?"

The opposite of love isn't hate. It's indifference. When your prospect is indifferent about your offer, then that's cause for concern. When he objects, he's engaged.

One of my favorite clients told me 15 years ago that he didn't believe in training. Each year I asked for his business, and each year he said "no." After I gave his team a freebie talk one afternoon, his sales numbers went up. He finally hired me and we've done projects together ever since. He still greets me to this day by saying: "You know I don't believe in training—can you help us script our new group presentation?" Sometimes when you know what customers *don't* want, you can better gauge what they *do* want.

4. **No makes you listen.**

When I first started selling, I decided to learn rebuttals for every possible objection the customer could throw at me. I became an objection fighter, a gladiator. It wasn't until I watched my mentor handle objections that I learned my approach was inappropriate. By answering them instantly, I was in effect proving the customer wrong. I was invalidating their concerns rather than welcoming them. When the customer feels shut down every time they express a concern, they stop telling you their concerns.

One of my best sales victories came after Marriott put me in charge of a new product and transferred me to Park City. It was my job to meet with the real estate community, many of whom had a negative view of vacation ownership (the euphemism used for time share) because of companies that overpromised and pressured people in the past.

"Just talk to them so they don't hate us," my boss said. "That's all you have to do."

I made friends with the biggest broker in town, Bill Cutler. He invited me into his Thursday morning weekly meeting to give a presentation to his 240 realtors.

I'll never forget it. There I was—new to town with all the sales hotshots folding their arms and practically throwing darts at me. I stepped to the front of the room and asked them to tell me everything they hate about vacation ownership.

Steve shouted out, "It's a horrible investment."

Carol chimed in, "It doesn't work!"

DJ said, "They're sold by tacky high-pressure salespeople."

They all laughed.

I took a deep yoga breath and wrote out in longhand all of their objections on a white board, and even egged them on.

"Tell me more," I said. "Keep them coming!"

I continued to write down all of the horrors locked up in their minds. I unleashed the beasts in their attics until they had exhausted their words.

I took a breath and said, "It's no secret timeshares had their problems. Bill Marriott knew that going into the business. That's why he created a program that was totally different—one that would protect his $8 billion brand. What I'm going to show you today is totally different from anything you've ever seen before."

Twenty minutes later, I had sold eight shares to the top brokers, including one to Bill Cutler!

5. **No is a negotiation tool.**

Many customers say "no" because salespeople have trained them to do so through the years. Put yourself in the place of the consumer. Do you walk into a car lot and say "yes" to the first offer? Have you ever said "no" to the first offer as a negotiation to get a better deal in the end? Of course you have—and your customers do it, too. Sometimes customers are testing you to see if your offer is the best offer.

When you hear a "no," don't ever change face. That's an expression one of my colleagues used to use to describe salespeople who would spend hours building a relationship only to pull a Jekyll and Hyde. They'd lash out at the customer at the first sound of a no. Your customer may either be testing the water to see if they can get a better price or testing you to see if you truly have their best interests at heart.

6. **No helps you hit stretch goals.**

Andrea Waltz, trainer, coach, and coauthor of *Go for No!*, counsels salespeople to *intentionally* increase their failure rate. When salespeople avoid the "no," they miss opportunities. She suggests setting "no goals" instead of "yes goals."

"No goals are especially critical when you're on a hot streak," she says.[4]

Let's say your goal for the week is three sales, and you achieve your target by Wednesday. The tendency is to take the next day off and bask in your glory. But if your goal is to go for 10 no's and after the three yes's you only got seven no's, you will aim for three more no's—and maybe get another yes!

I personally like setting "no" goals for my team. That way, even the less courageous people feel a sense of victory. After all, 20 no's is mission accomplished!

PUT IT INTO ACTION

Navigate the No's

In Chapter 9, I'll offer specific strategies for isolating and overcoming the kind of objections and excuses you'll hear during the closing process. The following techniques are useful whenever you hear "no." You'll get "no's" at every stage of the sales process:

* **Prospecting:** CEOs don't return your calls, your e-mails go unanswered, and people who promise to get back to you disappear like Houdini.
* **During your sales call:** Their arms are folded, their watch is more intriguing than your stories, and they suddenly *must* attend an urgent meeting.
* **Objections:** They read you a laundry list of what's wrong: why the competition is better, your product is too expensive, and your customer service is lousy.
* **The final close:** You've answered all of their questions and concerns, so you ask for an order. It seems it's the perfect solution for them, but they can't (or won't) buy today.

* **Listen fully before you respond.** Don't become defensive. I am always amused at salespeople who apologize or criticize customers when they disagree. Breathe. Let the customer finish their train of thought. Now ask yourself: Is this a deal killer? Many objections are valid—the customer just needs more information. Some test you to gauge if you will answer their concerns truthfully.

    When I hear an objection in the sales process, I listen fully. I validate the concern by saying, "I can absolutely see why you'd feel that way," or "That's a valid concern." I may even state their objection more strongly. "You certainly don't want to invest in a product that doesn't work for you. It sounds like you have enough on your plate." Then I wait for agreement. When I hear it, I'll confirm: "This is good. We're on the same page."

    You can't bring someone to your side of reasoning if you won't first move to theirs! Now, you can share more information, ideas, and an awesome rebuttal.

* **Answer a question with a question.** Listen fully and clarify the customer's "no" with a question. This is an extremely effective way to reduce ambiguity—just be careful not to overuse this technique. Here's an example of how a salesperson at a staffing agency used this technique:

    Buyer: Why don't you have a money-back guarantee?

    Seller: Have you had problems before?

    Buyer: Yes. Last month we brought in an executive assistant and in less than two weeks we knew she wouldn't work out.

    Seller: Do you have any other concerns?

    Buyer: Yes. I want to make certain you're vetting your employees appropriately.

    Instead of getting defensive about the lack of guarantee, the seller tried to identify the real issue. Once you know the customer concerns, you can address them. Had this seller not welcomed the prospect's fears and asked a clarifying question, he may not have ever uncovered the customer's real concern.

* **Remember that questions are often objections in disguise.** One of my business school students worked for an aircraft-part manufacturer attempting to close a major deal with the government. The customer asked, "How much testing did you do?"

  My student was taught to ask himself: What's the real concern here? What's the "no" or the barrier underneath the question? By doing so, he discovered that what the customer was *really* asking was: Is this model safe? Do we need to launch additional testing before bringing it to market?

  Again, think before you act. In sales, no never means no, which means you should never bulldoze your way through with a rebuttal. Instead, listen, analyze, and respond to the concerns the customers express and the concerns they may not even know to express.

* **Know when to isolate a "no."** You've had it happen before: customers that rattle off question after question, concern after concern. It sounds like an endless sea of "no's." Don't give up. Instead, ask a question that isolates the customer's concern and listen carefully for the response.

A hotel company that books large events and weddings was working with a very upscale client. One of their top salespeople, Natasha, had answered about 10 questions when the customer asked, "Do you allow pets?"

Instead of answering yes or no, she isolated the concern by asking, "Would that be important to you in your decision to secure a venue?"

The customer thought a moment and said it would be nice, but not essential.

Some questions aren't a "no" at all. You just need to isolate the deal breakers from the chatter.

Where Does Courage Live?

Getting thorough the "no's" in your life takes courage. But keep in mind that the word "courage" originates from the root "cor"—the Latin word for heart. When you care enough about your product, your customers, and yourself, your heart will outweigh your fear.

The Lion in *The Wizard of Oz* traveled far, risked his life, and defeated the Wicked Witch of the West in the hopes that when he reached the Emerald City, the great Oz would grant him courage. But when the curtain fell away, the wizard was revealed to be a little man speaking in a megaphone, frantically tugging at levers.[5]

It's all smoke and mirrors. Too often salespeople hope someone, *anyone*, will give them the answer. But no one will ever hand you a badge of courage unless you earn it—which is exactly what the Lion had already done on the way to meet Oz.

Courage isn't something that happens to you; it is generated by your actions. Courage must be practiced. If you wait to take action until the fear goes away, the inspiration will never come.

Strategies for Beating the Fear of Rejection

1. **Go for the standing ovation every time.**

   The ultimate downfall for most salespeople is their inability to handle rejection. But if you're going to make it in sales, you have to be able to take rejection—and lots of it. It's just that simple. My mentor told me a long time ago to count the number of "no's" I get and realize that each "no" simply moves you closer to a "yes."

   "Give each customer your best shot each time," he told me. "Never take a shortcut."

   Legendary actor Yul Brynner performed as King Monkut of Siam in the Broadway production of *The King and I* for an astounding 4,625 shows—each time to a standing ovation.

"When you are a pianist," Brynner explained, "you have an outside instrument that you learn to master through finger work and arduous exercises. . . . As an actor, you the artist have to perform on the most difficult instrument to master, that is, your own self—your physical and your emotional being."[6]

The great Joe DiMaggio was once asked why he gave his all even in statistically meaningless late season games, after the Yankees had been eliminated from the pennant race.

"There's always a kid who came to the game to see me play for the first time," he responded. "He deserves to see me give my all."[7]

You need to approach each call with the same level of professionalism and confidence. *Every audience deserves your best performance.*

2. **Look toward the end of the curve.**

My friend Anna is one of the greatest athletes I know. She mountain bikes 7,000 vertical feet in an afternoon, leads rock climbs in Yosemite, and runs intervals in the park—for fun. Just six weeks after Anna underwent major surgery, we went mountain biking, but for once she was the one who couldn't keep up.

That's when I gave Anna the same advice that she had given me just weeks earlier. "Always look at where you want to go. If you only gaze right in front of you, you'll lose your balance. There's nothing you can do about it anyway. Look ahead to where you want to be."

Set goals into the future. If you don't reach them, or if you hit an obstacle, look beyond where you are now to where you want to go. Tough people know that life is going to be hard, so they prepare themselves for hardship and remember where they're headed.

3. **No excuses.**

A few years ago, I had hats and T-shirts made for my employees and customers that said, "No Excuses." If a deal falls through, it doesn't matter why. The electric company doesn't care if you *almost* got the deal when it's time to pay the bill.

When it comes to prospecting and closing, "No never means no." Have tenacity. When you hear "no," go around, through, and on top of it in order to make the sale. Average sellers say things like "I left a message and he didn't call back," "I sent an e-mail, but didn't get an answer," and "She must not be interested."

Selling not only takes tenacity, but also creativity, a sense of humor, and an innate sense of how and when to change the emotional state of the customer to get their attention and earn their business.

These days, your customers are crazy busy and on information-overload. If their first response is "no," it may not be that they're not interested; it's just that *your priority isn't your customer's priority until you make it so*. Surprise, surprise! Getting in touch with them may be of number-one importance in your life, but about 50th in theirs . . . until you get through to them and convince them otherwise.

When prospecting, the last thing you want to do is continually approach the client in the same way with the same message. Try mixing up your approaches. For example:

* Send them a message on Twitter, Facebook, or LinkedIn in response to something they posted. Let them know you're listening.
* Send them a thought-provoking article that you think may benefit them or their business.
* If you're conducting business with a colleague or a competitor, make sure they receive a newsletter or a press release touting the benefits of your product or service along with a testimonial.
* Make friends with their assistant or coworker and secure an appointment through them.

* When sending a follow-up e-mail, make certain to speak to their dominant buying motives or business objectives.
* Send a poem. *Yes*, a poem! Let me explain.

I obtained one of my biggest contracts to date by sending a pizza and poem to a busy executive who simply wouldn't return my calls. His assistant repeatedly told me, "He's in a meeting." I thought, "Geez, this poor guy is always in a meeting. He probably never gets out for a walk or ducks out at lunch for a workout. I'm not sure he even eats!"

"Has he eaten lunch yet?" I asked his assistant.

"No."

"What's the best pizza place around?" I asked.

"Pauli's, just down the street."

"Great," I replied. "I'm going to buy Matt a pizza and have it sent to the office. I'll order enough for everyone. Oh, and I'm going to fax a poem to you. Do you mind attaching it to the pizza box for me before you bring him the pizza?" She giggled and did as I asked. The poem read:

Is it sunny or is it raining?
The weather's always good with online training.
I know you're busy playing business and banker
But isn't it time we set down our anchor?
Think of the increased volume it will yield
The consistent messaging out in the field.
So when you're done with that last pepperoni
Pick up the phone and let's make some money!

Did I hear back? You guessed it! I got a call in 90 minutes. It ended up in a very large deal.

I've always had *chutzpah*. I suppose it takes quite a bit of that to stand out in today's environment. When I first started my training company, I was on the phone 10 hours a day. I called every CEO I knew who was a possible client and offered to perform a trial seminar for free. "All I ask is that you're in the room for at least one hour," I told them. "If you like it, book me at full price. If not, you've got nothing to lose."

4. **Celebrate the no's.**

Have you heard of the Moonshot Factory? It's a part of Google where the workers are applauded, revered, and even given bonuses for, well, failure. The name of the innovation lab originates from John F. Kennedy's dream of putting a person on the moon. The very use of the words "moonshot" and "factory" supports the notion that dreams aren't just visions: They're *visions* with a *strategy*. But the idea behind the Moonshot Factory isn't simply to push the limits of what's possible—it's the building of a culture that intentionally chases after failure.

To paraphrase Astro Teller, who runs the factory, employees spend most of their time trying to break things and determine what's not working. The company views cancelled projects as the catalyst to innovation. In fact, employees that end projects receive bonus money and vacations![8]

I realize not every company has the ability to give bonuses to people for plans and programs that don't work. And, there's also much debate about whether the Factory will be a success for Google. Their losses are currently in the hundreds of millions!

But the idea behind the Factory is provocative and inspiring. We can remind ourselves that each time we try an approach that doesn't work, we can move closer to what does work. I also find that when we admit mistakes or even weaknesses, it simply makes us look and feel more confident. Reframe how you perceive your failures. When you lose a sale or have a lousy quarter, you learn what doesn't work. You save time and energy by learning what not to do in the future.

5. **Make it a game.**

I made it a game to see how many "no's" I could get, knowing that each objection simply meant the client needed more information, or different information, or they simply hadn't yet experienced me live. Then I figured out how to turn the no into a yes, no matter how long it took. Some "no's" took 10 years, maybe 15. I just never take it personally. When you're in sales, no never means no. That doesn't mean you'll always end up with a deal, but if you're wise you'll always end up with a lesson.

Find a way—think creatively—and if you don't get the deal today, know that someday you might.

In the next chapter, I'll show you the elements of establishing trust. Do they work? Trust me. Every time.

CHAPTER 5

Trust Begins With Empathy

Universal Truth #5: Trust is born of empathy, integrity, reliability, and competency. You need all four traits, but without connecting on an empathetic level, you won't have a chance to demonstrate the other three. Empathy is the first building block of trust. We can't pretend to have empathy. Empathy is not about shifting the conversation to what you want to say or judging your customer. It's about being fully engaged and present to someone else's emotions.

Empathy: The First Building Block of Trust

We've explored the idea that all decisions are emotional. In this chapter, we're going to talk about getting the customer to actually trust you, and trust you enough to reveal their emotional drivers. Trust of this breed requires empathy and a skill I call "wholehearted listening." When you truly listen, understand, and care, customers will open up to you. They will show you exactly how to sell to them. It's up to you to listen to the cues they offer.

First, let's understand what empathy means. It doesn't mean feeling sorry for the other person. Empathy literally means feeling *with* the other person—understanding what he or she is feeling at that moment. It means setting aside our own desires, fears, and even prejudices as we relate to another person.

When your doctor listens to your heartbeat with her stethoscope, do you think she's thinking about herself? Not if she's a true professional. She wants to understand your inner world, so she stays entirely focused on that task. We salespeople don't use stethoscopes. But we are indeed listening to the heart of our prospects. When we shift our focus from what we want out of a transaction (victory, commission, the trip to Jamaica in the sales contest) to what the prospect wants, magic happens.

Anger Waiting to Happen

Long ago, early in my career, I was trying to sell a lovely three-bedroom villa to a semi-affluent family man named George Mills. George and his family drove from Colorado to the villa—a four-and-a-half hour trip, mind you—but when they arrived, George sought me out to shout at me. The room they were staying in was filthy, he loudly complained.

I admit I only half-listened, and scurried downstairs to do my own share of complaining.

I tried to convince my manager, Greg, to send this horrible, angry man away, but he wouldn't. Instead, Greg asked me a few questions.

"What does this 'angry man' do for a living?"

"He's a school principal," I replied.

"Do you think he might have problems at work?"

"He did seem pretty upset."

But why should that be my problem, I wondered?

And it suddenly occurred to me—*maybe he's under a lot of pressure.* My Aunt June had worked at a school, and after years of loyal service, she was replaced by a woman half her age.

"Might he have problems in his personal life?" Greg said.

"The older daughter seems like a handful."

Teenagers—what a nightmare! I knew that from babysitting my nieces for just a few hours. George had three of them, full time!

"Sometimes people are just angry," Greg said. "They're what I call 'anger waiting to happen.' It has nothing to do with you. You just happened to be there."

Instead of thinking about my lost sale, I started to think how George must have felt. I felt ashamed.

I rushed back up to the Mills family. I apologized on behalf of the company for the poor service. I offered them cold drinks. I suggested George write a letter to the president of the company describing the mishap, while I personally cleaned his unit, because the housecleaning staff had left for the evening.

(As it turned out, the room wasn't that messy. The housecleaning staff had just left the garbage bag at the entrance by mistake.)

As I turned to find some stationery, Mr. Mills put down his pipe, looked up at me, and exclaimed: "You're a saleswoman, not a housekeeper!"

"Same company," I replied.

"Well, it's really not that bad," he admitted.

I went through each step of my sales process as I had been taught. Mostly, I listened, and I came to like and respect him.

One hour later, Mr. Mills purchased one of our largest packages.

And here's the kicker: He told all of his friends about it for the next five years. They all said, "If Millsy bought one of those, it's got to be good. He's such a crabapple!" I ended up selling to several of them, as well.

That day, I learned an important lesson about empathy:

It's much easier to make a sale if you listen with your heart. I could have argued with George Mills over facts. After all, his room wasn't technically "filthy." But empathy doesn't begin with facts or data. It has nothing to do with being right.

In her popular TED Talk, political commentator Sally Kohn calls for people to worry less about political correctness and more about *emotional correctness*.[1] In other words, in life, people disagree—whether it's about politics, raising children, or committing to a purchase. It's more important to understand how someone *feels* rather than what they say.

Replace the Hard Sell With the Heart Sell

Let's be honest. It's tough to generate genuine empathy with the couple that is rude, or the CEO who brushes you off. It's hard sometimes to avoid seeing your customers as dollar signs, especially if your own finances are shaky. Yet, when you make an effort to genuinely care and replace the "hard sell" with the "heart sell," everything changes.

You have probably been told that to earn trust, you have to get your customers to like you. That's backward. Earning someone's trust doesn't start with getting customers to like you—it begins with empathy, with *you* caring about *them*. Trust follows empathy. Otherwise, we're just another salesperson with a hand in our prospect's pocket.

So how do we become more empathetic? We start by establishing rapport. Rapport is a precursor to empathy. You've almost certainly heard about establishing rapport in sales seminars you've taken. In my experience, most salespeople are taught to view rapport simply as a box to check. Match and mirror. Pace. That's all useful, but where's the humanity that animates this new relationship with your prospect?

On its own, *rapport isn't enough to build strong trust*. I won't leave my kids with you just because I like you. You need to pay attention to the actual person across from you, not just the imaginary construct of a person you think they are. You need to listen with your eyes, your ears, and especially your heart. Empathizing with another's point of view is the cornerstone of trust.

Ramp Up Your Rapport-Building Skills

Salespeople don't always know how to build rapport with customers. Sometimes I find they want to build deeper rapport with customers, but they lack the know-how. They don't know how to maintain a natural conversation, they don't know how to understand (and care about) another person's point of view, and they don't know how to listen for unspoken emotions and objections. They don't understand the deep mysteries common to each of us, and they can't imagine creating the foundation of a trusting relationship. A lack of abilities isn't always the problem; a lack of awareness and failure to learn and practice are.

The following is a list of eight concepts to remember when building rapport. Start to incorporate these techniques during your warm-up step: When you can build rapport with people in the first moments of a sales call, you transform skepticism and anxiety into trust and anticipation.

1. **Give them your credit card.**

    In my first true sales job, customers who made same-day decisions were rewarded with special bonuses. We'd make our best offer to customers and hope they'd buy on the spot.

    We soon realized that many people wanted to think about the offer during lunch. One of my colleagues insisted that his customers leave their credit card to keep the offer open. He expected them to return with a "yes" or "no" decision. Unfortunately, this distrust often resulted in what the salesperson most feared: no deal.

    I took the opposite approach. When my customer asked to discuss the proposal during lunch, I assured them, "Please, be my guest. Right across the street there's a cute café called the Sweet Onion. Take my credit card and I'll see you when you get back."

    Now, you may be thinking, "Whoa, that will cost me a fortune. What if they don't buy?" The truth is, those customers almost always returned and purchased.

    Think about it; if I do something nice for you, you'll have a deep psychological urge to return the favor. If I pick up the bill for dinner this time, you're likely to pick up the tab next time. Trust works the same way.

    A prime example of this involves the band Radiohead. In 2007, musicians were freaking out because young people were illegally downloading their music, bypassing the record companies and the artists. Rather than playing the victim or feeling resentful, Radiohead took a different tack. They put their album *In Rainbows* on their website with instructions on how to download it. Instead of a price, buyers saw a question mark, and then the prompt:

"It's up to you."

Not only did the tactic create a ton of buzz, Radiohead "made more money before *In Rainbows* was physically released than they made in total on [their ironically titled previous album] *Hail to the Thief.*"[2]

I'm not saying you should give all your products away for free or spend time with unqualified prospects (or even buy them lunch!). The point is that earning trust starts with you. We can't guarantee every customer will trust us, but we *can* begin by trusting them and becoming the kind of people worthy of earning their trust.

2. **Be interested in their battles.**

Each time you meet a prospect, find at least one positive character trait and offer a sincere compliment. Don't just say "Hey, that's a cool jacket," or "Wow, what a beautiful bracelet!" These are surface-level details that don't reflect the true nature of your prospect. Is he patient with his kids? Is he funny? Is her work fascinating? If you can appreciate the things your prospects most value about themselves, you're halfway to the sale.

Admittedly, finding something to like can sometimes be difficult. Our usual tendency is to judge. Get past that initial impulse and find something genuinely admirable. This allows you to build a relationship with a customer while enriching your own life.

For example, I checked into my first spa resort when I was 32 and single. The dinner hall was filled with happy couples. The captain's table, on the other hand, was where people mingled.

Each night I made a decision. I had nothing in common with the captain and his crew. They didn't look like me. They weren't my age. I'd never wear that hat! Maybe I should sit alone?

Each night, however, I forced myself to sit at the captain's table, and each night flew by. I listened to my tablemates' stories, and I always found something to admire or respect about them. Everyone has a story. We are told to "Be kind, for everyone you meet is fighting a great battle." Or as Zig Ziglar used to say, "If you treat everyone as if they're hurting, you're probably treating everyone the right way."[3]

Though our stories may vary, when we take the time, we often discover our struggles are the same.

3. **Love the unlovable.**

Some people are more difficult to love than others. If you've seen *Shrek*, you may remember the scene when Donkey tries to build a relationship with Shrek, even though Shrek is an ogre. Shrek is dismissive and uninterested in Donkey, but Donkey is persistent. He tells Shrek "You know what I like about you, Shrek? You got that kind of I-don't-care-what-nobody-thinks-of-me thing. I like that."[4]

My mentor once told me, "It's easy to love the loveable: the rich, the pretty, and the qualified." It's more difficult to love the ogres. But keep in mind: *The way people act and who they can become are two different things. And even ogres have bank accounts and credit cards.*

When we label people, prejudge, or otherwise classify them, we deny them and ourselves the opportunity for growth. Had I simply labeled George Mills a jerk, I never would have made the sale. Believing in another person's potential is the growth mindset at work. If you look at people in terms of their potential rather than in terms of their current actions, you will build better relationships in the sales room, the boardroom, and your living room.

Remember that labels are for shirts, not human beings.

4. **Notice the purple hats.**

What about the people who present themselves in ways that seem designed to circumvent your every attempt at taking them seriously? For example, the teacher in a purple hat with feathers, the senior vice president dripping in gold and Gucci, and the weight lifter popping out of his tank top—how are you supposed to approach them?

You've probably heard the expression, "We need to talk about the elephant in the room"? Think of it like this: If I invite you to our home in Park City, Utah, for dinner, and there in the foyer is a circus elephant squatting next to the grand piano, would you say anything? If you don't, it's going to be awkward for both of us. The elephant is so obviously unusual.

The elephant sparks tension in the process of creating an open, authentic relationship—but we can reduce the tension simply by acknowledging its presence. People wearing wild outfits, or guests who are dressed to the nines at a fishing cottage, are individuals who want to be seen, noticed, and admired.

When you meet someone whose appearance shouts, "Look at me!" you have one option. You have to look. You have to comment. "Nice hat! Where'd you get those feathers?" or "How long did it take you to get 46 tattoos?" Don't project your own discomfort with their appearance onto them. They chose their clothing. They aren't afraid of it. Why should you be?

Selling would be so easy if we only had to sell to people with our appearance, background, and tastes. But that's not how the game is played.

5. **Don't be a one-up-man (or woman).**

My parents had an acquaintance that my brother and I called Herb One-Up-Man, because Herb had a particularly annoying habit. For instance, when my dad shared how he'd surprised my mother with a trip to the Big Island of Hawaii for her birthday, Herb broke in mid-sentence: "Hawaii's beautiful. Good choice.

We have a second home there. By the way, I won't make it to the board meeting next Wednesday—we'll be in the Maldives scuba diving. Do you mind taking extra good notes, Lloyd?"

Herb had an amazing knack for redirecting anyone's sentence, whatever the topic, into an opportunity for him to boast about his New York penthouse, his negotiating prowess, or his vast wine collection.

I once watched a customer proudly share his son's acceptance to Boston College only to be one-upped by a saleswoman who remarked that her daughter received a full scholarship to Harvard. It was sad, and I felt really bad for the man whose son's achievement was overshadowed by someone who just sucked all the attention from the room.

Don't compete with your prospect. Even if you win the one-upmanship battle, you still lose the sale.

6. **Value their time and share their values.**

A few months ago, my husband and I made a decision to replace what he lovingly called his "shopping cart of a vehicle" with a new truck. He made an appointment with a salesperson named Chuck, but assured me on the ride to the dealership that he would price-shop before making a purchase.

But Chuck had done his homework. When he greeted us, the first words out of his mouth were, "Congratulations." He complimented my husband on his work at a charitable organization that focused on helping people with mental and physical disabilities. Chuck told us he had a child with autism, and my husband offered to put Chuck in touch with people at the organization.

Not only did Chuck do his research, but he connected to something my husband valued. By talking about something they both cared about, Chuck deepened the connection—and it empowered my husband to be more than just a passive customer.

If you are in a position where you are prospecting customers or you know who they are in advance, you must take the time to conduct research. The more you learn about them, the more you're telling them that you value them and think they're important.

Five minutes into his conversation with Chuck, my husband said, "It looks like they have a nice selection here." We left with a sparkling new Silverado 4×4. I'm sure that comes as no surprise to you!

7. **Go deeper.**

I vividly recall a cartoon of a salesperson greeting three different prospects in a day:

* "You're from New York? How about that? Me too! How 'bout them Mets!"
* "You're from San Francisco? What a coincidence, love it. Me too."
* "Atlanta? Y'all, we're neighbors!"

Although these remarks may build surface-level relationships, they don't create an authentic bond. Real rapport is created when we share common values and ideas, not simply common interests or places of origin. I heard a great story in one of my seminars about Jack, a regional manager who had been trying unsuccessfully to get a renewal on a major software account for the past couple of years. He had sent seven different sales representatives to meet with Phil, the head honcho, and not one of them could land the deal.

The eighth rep, Jack, finally succeeded. As it turned out, Jack was a veteran from the Vietnam War. When he met with Phil, who had also been in 'Nam, they engaged in the usual bit of small talk, but after about 25 minutes, Jack looked Phil in the eyes, patted him on the shoulder, and with all the sincerity you can imagine, said "Welcome home, man." The two soldiers teared up and embraced, and the account was won.

When building rapport with your clients, do your best to discuss things you have in common that touch the heart: mutual causes such as children, education, health, animals, military service, and nature. Of course, be careful discussing religion and politics. Share photos, stories, and ideas that center on values over vocations. Go beyond the usual "Is that your sailfish?" or empty chatter about the local sports team's chances. Trust is deepened when we share similar values and beliefs.

8. **Let them talk about themselves.**

When I was single, a friend suggested I meet a man whom she described as utterly fascinating. Chaz arrived in a blue convertible and treated me to Italian food for lunch. He told me about the five books he'd published. He described his real estate holdings. Eventually, he went on to discuss his celebrity contacts.

I listened, asked questions when he paused for air, and leaned forward. I was the perfect listener. Unfortunately, he was a perfect bore. An hour went by, and I hadn't gotten a word in edgewise. Not for lack of trying. Chaz drove me home and escorted me to my front door, but I was pretty sure that there was no chemistry there. Then he looked me deep in the eyes, paused, and said, "I just want to tell you: You're the most fascinating woman I've ever met!"

He didn't get inside.

He didn't get a second date, either.

We trust the people who take the time to get to know us. But giving someone else the floor is difficult to do. Research from the *Harvard Business Review* shows that on average, people spend 60 percent of their time talking about themselves, a number that increases to 80 percent on social media.[5]

The Greek philosopher Epictetus said it first: "We have two ears and one mouth so that we can listen twice as much as we speak." Obviously, Epictetus never saw Instagram. The reality is more complex, but this much is true: When we talk about ourselves, we experience increased activity in the area of the brain associated with motivation and reward. These are the same pleasure centers associated with good food, cocaine, and sex. Simply put, we default to *look at me* mode because it feels so damn good.

One of the hardest things for salespeople to do is to listen more than talk. But listening is key to developing empathy, a deeper connection and, eventually, the sale.

But What if I Can't Find Common Ground?

Salespeople feel frustrated when they can't find common ground. Desperately seeking similar interests, they fire off questions and move from topic to topic. "Do you like to camp? Where are you from? How long have you been in this business?" When you default to this behavior, the customer feels disregarded; you're saying, "I don't care what your answers are, so I don't care about you."

Stanford lecturer and speaking coach Lee Eisler devised a strategy to dig deeper and find commonalities, even when doing so seems impossible.[6] Suppose you meet a prospect whose interests differ wildly from yours. You can still create common ground by moving beyond the obvious questions.

For example:

Seller: What do you like to do for fun?

Prospect: Hunt.

Seller (*oh, God, I'm a vegan*): So! What do you like about hunting?

Prospect: Getting away from it all. Being outdoors.

Seller: Ah, me too. I go camping a few times every summer. What do you like about the outdoors?

Prospect: It makes me feel alive and sort of peaceful at the same time.

Seller (thoughtful pause): Yes, me too. . . . I definitely feel that when I'm hiking.

This savvy seller found commonality in the *qualities* and *sentiment* of the activity the customer enjoyed, rather than just in the activity. Don't mention your life membership in PETA, and maybe he won't talk about the NRA. You aren't being hypocritical; you're simply exercising good judgment.

Try this yourself. The next time you meet someone, a customer or a new acquaintance, start by determining the interests you have in common with them—usually things like family, travel, pets, mutual acquaintances, or activities. If you don't have mutual interests (and even if you do), how can you still achieve a deeper communication? Be curious. Ask what they do and, more importantly, *why they do it*. Seek out the feelings behind their interests.

Learn Wholehearted Listening

Ken Petress, a professor of communication at the University of Maine, says, "Unlike hearing, which is a physiological passive activity, listening is an active cognitive process."[7]

In its simplest terms, real empathy involves listening and understanding your customer's heart, mind, soul, and emotions. It's about putting your judgments aside and being present to their hopes, fears, beliefs, and needs. It's about understanding what makes their life worth living.

How well do you feel you listen? In their book *Are You Really Listening?* authors Paul Donoghue and Mary Siegel comment, "Everyone wants to be understood, but few people feel they are. Surprisingly, most people think that they are good listeners."[8]

I'm often called upon to assess salespeople within an organization. I can size up a salesperson and tell if a sale is going to go down before the salesperson ever discusses his offering—I just notice who is doing most of the talking.

A lot of people think that listening and hearing are the same. They are most assuredly not. Hearing is passive; it doesn't transform us. It doesn't stir our deeper emotions or bring us any real insights. Real listening, on the other hand, demands that we place our own filters and prejudices aside. It requires discipline. It's what I call "wholehearted listening."

Salespeople rarely listen wholeheartedly. Our tendency often is to think of what we want to say next, and interrupt because we're impatient to offer our own opinions—and because, deep down, we couldn't care less what the prospect has to say prior to "I'll take it." Wholehearted listening is different. It involves understanding people the way they want to be understood. It's what salespeople must do to show empathy and win deals. It short, it takes energy—lots of it.

The Three Dimensions of Listening

What people say and what they feel don't always mesh. So how can you know how to respond? You can see it in their body language. You can hear it in their tone. I once heard a saying, "If all three don't agree, they're lying to me"—"all three" meaning words, body language, and tonality.

An artist friend was showing her latest oil paintings to the owner of a fine art gallery. The owner assured her he was interested, but he sat back with crossed arms and continually looked above her head. It was obvious that he had no intention of calling her back. Luckily, she saw the disconnect and took her work elsewhere.

Top sellers know when customers aren't telling them the whole story.

The Said, the Unsaid, and the Unsayable

Acclaimed screenwriting teacher Robert McKee makes a distinction between the different types of dialogue. I've found this idea is also extremely useful when applied to listening skills. In his book *Dialogue*, McKee reminds us that communication is complex. Words are only the surface. Great dialogue in a media production, he says, contains these three dimensions:

* **The said**: What people choose to say.
* **The unsaid**: What people are feeling, but may not tell you in words.
* **The unsayable**: The subconscious urges and desires people cannot express in words because they aren't even aware of them.[9]

When you're listening to your customers, think of these three dimensions and watch what happens to your ability to pay close attention and empathize. Ask yourself: What is my customer feeling that she's not telling me? What's he thinking that he may not even know consciously?

Notice that both you and the customer will engage in one or more of these three dimensions during every interaction. Like the audience in a play or the reader of fiction, think of yourself as the audience and your client as the actor reciting the majority of the dialogue. The more engaged you are in what he or she is saying, the more engaged they will feel. Pay attention not only to what is said, but also to what isn't.

THE FIRST DIMENSION OF LISTENING: THE SAID

At this level of listening, you simply listen to the other person's words. You're not attuned to body language because you're busy thinking about what to say next. Similarly, your prospect may not feel "felt" yet, so they'll rush to finish.

The following are observable signs indicating either you or your prospects are stuck in the first dimension of listening:

* Turning away and looking around at what else is happening.
* Repeatedly checking your watch, phone, etc.
* Interrupting.
* Fidgeting, tapping, and other signs of restlessness.
* Saying nothing to engage the speaker in further conversation.

THE SECOND DIMENSION OF LISTENING: THE UNSAID

At this level, you begin to uncover nonverbal cues. You not only notice the other person's words, but you observe their body language and uncover the emotion behind the words. You listen with your ears, but also with your eyes. You encourage the prospect to provide more information, to disclose more about the issue and themselves. The prospect, feeling heard, begins to share more details. He may start to reveal fears, desires, and beliefs.

The following are observable signs indicating you or your prospects are using second-dimension listening skills:

* Showing involvement in what is being said, that is, responding appropriately.

- Asking questions and seeking more information; for example, "Tell me more."
- Forward-leaning body language.
- Using good eye contact.
- Allowing for pauses and even intermittent silence.

THE THIRD DIMENSION OF LISTENING: THE UNSAYABLE

At this level, you focus your complete attention on the speaker and your concentration is so intense that you capture both content and intent. You refrain from prejudging or rejecting what you hear. You feel "in the zone" or "on the same wave length." You are so engaged that you feel an emotional shift as someone shares information, ideas, and beliefs with you. This is what I refer to as "wholehearted listening."

The following are observable signs indicating you or your prospects are using wholehearted listening skills:

- Allowing for long pauses in between thoughts.
- Heads nodding in agreement.
- Letting the other person finish each train of thought.
- Feeling a shift in your emotional state.
- Allowing yourself to feel the other person's pain, joy, and excitement.

The chart on page 121 will help you assess how well you listen and how well your customers are listening to you.

To relate effectively with a prospect, a customer, our boss, our neighbor, or our spouse, we must learn wholehearted listening. This requires discipline and practice. It involves the emotional intelligence skills of patience and curiosity. It requires the desire to understand *who* another person is and what makes his life worth living. It's much easier to default into talking about facts than it is to muster the strength to feel what's inside someone's heart.

People are usually gentler on the inside than they are on the outside. We hide our true selves behind false bravado. Get to know the real person, not who you think they are or who you pretend to be. This is the first step

Listening Skills Checklist

Listening Skills	Most of the time	Frequently	Occasionally	Almost Never
1. Do you sometimes tune out people who don't agree with you or don't say what you want to hear?				
2. Do you concentrate on what the speaker is saying even when you're not interested?				
3. Do you get impatient with those with different speech patterns than your own? For example, talk slower, faster or in a whiney voice?				
4. Do you assume you know what the speaker is going to say and stop listening?				
5. Do you think about how you're going to refute their objection rather than allowing them to elaborate on it?				
6. Do you stop asking questions as soon as you hear their Dominant Buying Motive rather than letting them talk and feel more about it?				
7. Do you repeat in your own words what the speaker just said?				
8. Do you look in the eyes of the person who is speaking?				
9. Do you concentrate on the person's meaning, not just the words?				

continued

Listening Skills	Most of the time	Frequently	Occasionally	Almost Never
10. Do you know which words and phrases have an emotional trigger for you?				
11. Do you know which words and phrases have an emotional trigger for them?				
12. Do you plan the best time to say what you want to say?				
13. Do you daydream while the speaker is talking?				
14. Do you allow the other parties in the group to share their thoughts and feelings as well?				
15. Do you ask what a word or concept means when you are not familiar with it?				
16. Do you give the appearance of listening when you aren't?				
17. Do you listen to the speaker without criticizing or judging?				
18. Do you allow the speaker to vent negative feelings or experiences with your product without becoming defensive?				
19. Do you restate what you believe you heard?				
20. Do you think about what you want to accomplish with your communication?				

toward building trust. But as I'll explore in the next chapter, demonstrating your reliability, integrity, and competence is key to implementing change and gaining customer commitment.

Although rapport and empathy get you in the door, reliability, competency, and integrity keep you there. And those topics are the subjects of our next chapter.

CHAPTER 6

Integrity Matters

Universal Truth #6: Once we cultivate true empathy, we find it impossible to lie to or cheat our customers—or anyone, for that matter, including ourselves. The word "sales" comes from the old English word for "give." When we sell, we must give. We can only maintain trust and enjoy enduring success when we cultivate honorable traits like reliability, competency, and integrity. Eventually, they become part of our character.

Why Aren't Your Customers Buying?

Do you know why your customers don't buy from you? Ken Allred, CEO of Primary Intelligence, does. His firm specializes in what's called "win-loss analysis"—that is, they analyze why sales opportunities are won or lost. Every year, Primary Intelligence interviews thousands of *buyers* about their purchase decisions—the sum of which typically totals more than $2 billion. Primary Intelligence did a discovery session with the salespeople and asked why they think their prospects didn't buy. Then they asked the *customers.*[1]

Guess what happened? The two responses couldn't be more different. The sellers claimed they lost the sale because the customer couldn't afford the product. But the buyers said they didn't buy because *it would take too much effort to make a change.*

One of the number-one reasons your customers don't buy from you has nothing to do with a competitor down the street and very little to do with big brands with cool new products. *They aren't buying from you because they prefer the status quo.*

This change in buyer behavior is a new one. But why? As a society we're suffering from information overload. We're busy and burnt-out. Time is the new currency—and we're all broke. Admittedly, my own life is a series of 1,246 unread e-mails (including yours—I promise I'll answer it soon), unclaimed insurance receipts, unpaid traffic tickets, missing pieces, and lost parts.

Your stressed-out customers simply can't fully grasp your new, complex offerings. They may like your product, and they may even see the value in it, but they don't have the bandwidth to understand what you're selling or why they even need it, so they're wary of making a change.

Be a "Helping Brand"

In the last chapter, we explored how to build a foundation for trust by establishing rapport and listening wholeheartedly. If your desire is to create a career for yourself rather than just showing up to work, you need to maintain and grow that trust.

Your customers are overwhelmed. Help make their lives easier—not with slick tricks and empty promises, but by proving yourself to be reliable, competent, and filled to the brim with integrity.

Don't expect your customers to trust you simply because you work for a reputable company or because you represent a sought-after product. Be transparent about your offering and the buying process itself. Not only does this openness help establish a connection, but it also makes things a lot easier for the customer. Strive to be a "helping brand"—a source of helpful information and insights—not simply another salesperson trying to make a quick buck.

Do you remember the scene in *Willy Wonka and the Chocolate Factory*? That's the one where the spoiled child Veruca Salt says to her daddy, "I want an Oompa Loompa now!"[2]

We want our problems to be fixed now. We want broken relationships mended and the pain of failure to be relieved. But when it comes to trust, there is no quick fix. The more you focus on empty promises and manipulative techniques, the more chronic your problems become. Trust begins with empathy—but to maintain it, you must demonstrate reliability, competency, and integrity. This requires hard work and constant discipline.

So in this chapter, we'll talk about how to get customers to trust you every time and with time.

Reliability: Little Things Equals Big Results

To this day, my mother is still my best friend. For as long as I can remember, whether she was picking me up from school or driving the kids to the mall, her motto was "Five minutes early is on time." Mom was, and still is, reliable. Because of her good example, I define reliability as *the ability to make and keep promises in a consistent basis*. Reliability, repeated with time, cements trust. Not only that, it will improve your outlook on life. When you keep your commitments, no matter how you may feel that day, you will see a huge shift in your mood.

Reliability is about:

* Being prepared and on time.
* Keeping your word.
* Wrapping up the end of your sales process with the same fervor you brought to the beginning of the process.
* Working through problems and ideas even after the sale is made.
* Doing more than you're asked to do.
* Being accountable.
* Sustained excellence in performance.

We use the word *reliable* to refer to something or someone who's dependable and whom we can count on. We might call an athlete reliable if he gives

127

his best performance game after game. Reliability gives your customers a certainty that you will deliver as promised and on time. It lets them know you will stand by what you sell them. It takes the fear out of changing vendors or trying something new.

In 1965, Frederick Smith, a Yale university graduate, wrote his term paper about the logistical challenges facing firms in the IT industry. His thesis was that delivery of essential products was too slow. He proposed a system of delivery to accommodate time-sensitive shipments such as medicine and computer parts. Smith's professor, not seeing the vision, gave Smith a C on the paper. However, Smith wasn't deterred and started the company anyway. Even though a *Yale Business School professor* told him it was a bad idea! In April of 1973, Federal Express was born.[3] FedEx revolutionized global business by offering two things: speed and reliability.

Can you imagine FedEx or Domino's Pizza staying in business if they didn't guarantee on-time delivery? Would you buy your coffee at Starbucks if your latte tasted different each time? What if each morning someone at the counter tried a new recipe or threw in a little cinnamon from his own spice drawer?

Most successful companies today made names for themselves not by making grand impossible promises, but by making simple promises and sticking to them. You, too, can build a reputation for reliability by committing to the following practices:

1. **Do what you say you're going to do.**
   * If you offer to send a brochure, do it.
   * If you offer a snack, serve it.
   * When you meet someone and say you'll follow up, do so— the next day.
   * If you say you're going to solve a customer issue, as Larry the Cable Guy says, "Get 'er done."

2. **Be responsive.**

   After three months of negotiating, my husband and I finally agreed upon a landscaping firm. They had great Yelp reviews and a reputation for quality work. We liked the owner. He listened to our needs. We shared common beliefs. He, too, has children in middle school and understood the need for boys to play outside. He seemed to understand how hard it is to juggle work, family, and community, which is what my husband and I deal with every day. In short, he "got" us as people.

Now, I understand very little about the technicalities of landscaping. All the talk about galvanized pipes, hunter heads, and gravel sump sounded like blah, blah, blah to me. I didn't need to get it. I knew *he* got *me*.

We agreed on the drawings, shook hands, and were excited to get started. But he neglected to call us back. It was impossible to reach him by phone. The contract arrived three weeks late. The rapport was there, the empathy was there, but because he was unreliable, he lost out trust. We sought out another firm.

These days, responsiveness is an unspoken expectation:

* Answer e-mails, phone calls, and texts within 24 hours.
* If you can't fix it now, assure your client you are working on it. Keep them informed.
* Respond to customers in their preferred mode of communication. Some prefer text, others e-mail, and some actually still like to meet for coffee or a cupcake!

3. **Make the right kind of promises.**

   Be careful about the promises you make. This has always been a problem for me. I find that I offer to take on more tasks that I can possibly accomplish. I often don't realize how long tasks take until after I've committed to them. By doing this I create unnecessary stress and frustration—not to mention unpaid traffic tickets and a messy kitchen.

   * Keep those promises that you make but, just as important, be judicious not to make too many.
   * If you find yourself unable to fulfill a promise, create a new agreement with the person you made it with. Be proactive about this; follow-though is key.

The idea isn't to make as few promises as possible, but to make the *right kind* of promises. When you make a promise to a customer, it might seem difficult to keep, but I can assure you that without any promises, you will have no customers.

4. **Welcome to my hometown of Guadalajara!**

Reliability in any relationship starts with setting realistic expectations. It's far more important for customers to have a realistic expectation of how your product works than for you to deliver a dazzling explanation of how you'd like it to work. Unfortunately, too many salespeople exaggerate product benefits or simply fail to explain what the customer should expect next. Failing to do either diminishes trust. Moreover, if you don't explain what customers should expect, there's a good chance that they'll feel uncertainty and fear.

When my friend Dave got married, he and his wife went to Mexico for their honeymoon. Now, Dave's terrified of flying—but he'd never told anyone about his fear, not even his new bride. So after boarding a tiny plane, Dave put on a brave face (and pounded down a few drinks from a flask) and did his best to stay calm.

"Take off, take off, take off," he thought as the plane sat on the runway.

Finally, the plane began to climb and climb—to 12,000 feet, 14,000—and, then, all of a sudden it started to go down and down. And down.

Dave felt sick. As the little plane flew down so far that he could see the little town below close up, he thought, "Oh my gosh, this is terrible. This is how my life is going to end! We haven't even had a baby."

Then, about three minutes later, the pilot announced, "I hope you like my hometown of Guadalajara! I just wanted to show you where I grew up!"

Had the pilot shared his flight plan with the passengers first, no one would have been scared, much less terrified. Can you imagine going to a doctor's office and getting poked and prodded without any explanation? That's what you're doing to your customers when you simply launch into a product pitch or fire off questions before you've told them where they're going.

A well-crafted statement of intent not only lets customers know exactly what to expect during your sales call, but sticking to it is one of the simplest ways to prove your reliability.

Craft Your Statement of Intent

This short statement (think one to three minutes) reduces client apprehension and tells her what she can expect. Perform this step following your warm-up, or after your discovery and confirmation statement. My statement of intent for virtual training with a brand new prospect might sound something like this:

You may be wondering how long this demonstration is going to take, how much it costs, and whether it might integrate with your existing platform. I'll be answering those questions today, as well as any other questions you may have. To best respect your time, I'd like to ask you a few questions about your current training program—what's working and what's not—as it will help me to better tailor my presentation to your needs. Please feel free to ask me any questions and voice any concerns.

A statement of intent serves two purposes:

1. **It lets the customer know you're reliable.** You demonstrate your reliability when you make a plan and follow through on it. It might be a promise to stick to a time frame, fix a problem, or provide them with information. Small, consistent actions speak much louder than bold promises.
2. **It decreases the customer's inherent tension.** Unspoken anxiety and fear kills trust. Reduce this uncertainty by telling your customer what to expect—and stick to your plan.

PUT IT INTO ACTION

Six Elements of Your Statement of Intent

You can use the acronym EASTER to script your own statement of intent: *e*mpathy statement, *a*genda, *s*et up the discovery, *t*ake off the pressure, *e*xpectations, and *r*equest interaction.

1. **Empathy statement:** Begin by recognizing the customer's feelings. People won't always volunteer feelings of apprehension. However, if you can acknowledge the "unsaid" you will increase connection and credibility. Is she feeling curious, apprehensive, excited, or suspicious? Knowing what your customer is feeling and acknowledging it is your first step.

   Example: *You may be wondering how long this demonstration is going to take, how much it costs, and whether it will integrate with your existing platform.*

2. **Agenda:** Next, tell your customers exactly what to expect during the sales call:

Customers Are Wondering:	Tell Them:
• How long will this take?	• Ten minutes, two hours, "Depending on interest."
• What will we be doing today?	• We'll be assessing your needs, looking to see if there's interest today or in the future.
• Who will I meet with?	• You, you and your VP, a finance manager
• Is your product compatible with what I'm currently using?	• Our product is meant to replace/augment what you're using now. (It's easier to sell supplemental offers—people hate change!)
• What will I see?	• Property, art, solar panels, the latest software.
• Is this a high-pressure sales pitch?	• It's not (then make sure to let them off the hook gracefully).

3. **Set up the discovery:** You need to ask permission to perform a discovery. If the customer sees value in your offering and agrees, he's more likely to open up to you. Let him know you understand that his time is valuable. Tell him that asking questions helps you better zero in on the most important features of your offering.

    Example: *To best respect your time, I'd like to ask you a few questions about your current training program—what's working and what's not—as it will help me to better tailor my presentation to your needs.*

4. **Take off the pressure:** Make sure to always let the customer off the hook by telling him he's under no obligation to purchase. Avoid sales clichés such as:

    * **I'm going to show you something you've never seen before.** Unless you really are about to show someone a flying elephant, don't make these statements. How do you know what someone has or has not seen?

    * **I'm not here to sell you anything today.** Then why are you here? Just feeling lonely? Your therapist is on vacation?

        People love to buy, but hate to be sold. Instead of resorting to tired clichés, be honest.

    Example: *"No" is a perfectly fine answer. This may not work for you, and it may not be the right timing.*

5. **Expectations:** Depending on what you're selling, you may want to clearly articulate what your customer can expect from you. Do you have a special on right now? Incentives? Might you ask for another meeting? A one-day sale? Maybe their first-born?

    Here are some examples of how to set expectations:

    * *We do have 30-percent discounts today.*

    * *Your timing is perfect. We just received our new inventory and we're offering special incentives.*

6. **Request feedback:** Communication is a two-way street. Now that you've delivered your statement of intent, ask the customer how she feels about what you've said. People don't want to listen to a conversation; they want to be part of the conversation.

   Example: *Do you have any questions or concerns? I'd love some feedback.*

What if You Don't Know?

What do you do when your client asks for additional information or asks you a question and you don't know the answer? Responding with "I don't know, but I'll find out" isn't as acceptable today as it used to be. Why? Information is abundant. You *should* know.

But let's say you're just starting out in your industry. You're selling a pretty complex product—and it's even complicated to you. How might you best respond? Here are two ideas:

1. **Borrow credibility**: Tell the customer you will ask someone else. "That's a great question. I'm not 100 percent sure, but I can find out by . . . [give a time frame]."
2. **Share what you *do* know**: Answer the question with related information you *do* know (if it's helpful). "What I do know is that interest rates are much higher today than they were a few months ago, but let me check into your specific question."

Don't Forget: What's Your Intent?

Your customer is consciously and unconsciously scanning your face, listening to your tone, and assessing your motives. Is this person trustworthy? Does he want what's best for me? Think hard about your motives before delivering your statement of intent. I was taught to memorize mine. My mentor said I should be able to recite it backward and forward in my sleep.

In the armed services, soldiers are trained to assemble and disassemble their weapons in the dark for building muscle memory and confidence. It's the same thing in sales. When you deliver your presentation with confidence and from memory, you can tune into your prospect's feelings. Ask yourself: "How can I help this person? How do I want her to feel about doing business with me?" You can't hide your intent. To be true to yourself, focus outside yourself.

Competency: It's About More Than Just Your Product

You're expected to know your product. You're expected to know the nuances of how and why it works. But to earn trust and loyalty today, you need more than that. You must share insights and provide value beyond the product you're selling. Today's customers need you to educate them—not just sell them.

1. **Be irreplaceable.**

   Back to Primary Intelligence—the firm that studies why people buy. In a parallel study to the one I mentioned earlier, their analysts studied the competencies salespeople need today to move customers away from the status quo. In addition to professionalism and responsiveness, "knowledge of their industry" topped the charts.[4]

   This may seem intuitive, but today industry knowledge means more than it used to. Stay on top of trends and industry news and you can deliver to your customers fresh insights they might not find anywhere else.

   Remember, products today are complicated. Your customers are wondering:

   * How does this compare to similar products? Am I getting the best deal?
   * What else should I be thinking about?
   * Who's going to help me navigate when I don't understand something?
   * Why should I use this company when so many out there seem to do the same thing?

2. **Knowledge is power, but insights are king.**

A while back I met Jarrod. The 27-year-old son of an auto mechanic and a disabled mother, he won every competition in his region selling smart phones and Internet service. He was a regional trainer by age 23. His boss soon became his direct report (every salesperson's dream) as he climbed the ladder to success.

Jarrod was switching customers from flip phones to smart phones in 2011. With new Internet services such as fiber optics solutions and DSL lines up for grabs, the consumer had just enough information to be deeply confused. Jarrod sold his way to the top spot in the state ethically, while breaking every sales award in the company.

When I asked him about the secret to his accomplishments, Jarrod replied, "I'm a techie. I learn everything about my product. But more importantly, I learn everything about my competitor's products so that when the customer is confused or threatens to check out a competitor, I give them the information they need so they can make an informed decision."

There's so much you can learn about your product, your competition, and trends in your industry. If you don't keep up, you will inevitably be crushed by someone who does (someone like Jarrod, perhaps).

3. **Give them what the Internet can't.**

I've heard it a thousand times. Freaked-out salespeople claim that increased product options coupled with competition from the Internet are costing them sales.

"They can buy it cheaper on the Internet," they complain. What's my response?

So what? Make competency your competitive advantage.

Since when do you only shop for the cheapest option? On date night, do you only eat at Burger King? Or do you spend more (a heck of a lot more) for a really nice meal in a fine restaurant? Competent customer service means forming a genuine relationship, solving problems, and looking for opportunities to offer insights.

Consider this:

* In recent years, the use of travel agents has risen by 36 percent. Sure, you can look up the best photography trip in Iceland on the Internet, but sometimes it's much better to talk to Magda the travel agent about the exact inlets, hotels, and roadways that she and her clients find most compelling.
* Charlie, an Audi salesman in Salt Lake City, picks all of his customers up at the airport while their cars are getting serviced. He even has their vehicles detailed while they're out of town. "Some of these new salesmen have no idea," he says. "Today, it's all about taking care of your customers."
* George sells vacation ownership in Cabo San Lucas. He's no longer fazed when customers tell him they can vacation cheaper through Expedia. He highlights his company's concierge service and points out how their services will save them valuable time. Plus, he shows them secret snorkeling spots and makes them reservations at off-the-beaten-path restaurants. Even Google can't do that for you.

What can you offer that the Internet can't? Make a list. Start with service and connection. This list should give you a kick start:

* Tech support.
* Babysitting services.
* Restaurant recommendations.
* Your expertise.
* Advice.
* Great feeling during the sales experience.
* Connection.
* After-sale servicing.
* Friendship.

* A favor for their kids.
* Community: ability to meet others who bought the same product or service.

4. **Teach customers how to buy.**

Today's buyers need you to help them sort through the deluge of information and specifications regarding your product. Ask yourself, "What would I want to know if I was buying my genre of product? What things should I think about, worry about, and plan for?"

Buyers need to understand your sales process, but they also need you to steer them through their buying process. Help customers understand what to think about when purchasing a product like yours. Yes, I said *like yours*. Whether they buy from you or not, help buyers navigate the minefield in front of them. Take the effort out of their decision-making, and make buying from you a snap.

For example, when I talk to customers about our learning software, I don't merely focus on the features and benefits of my system. Rather, I tell them what to consider when purchasing *any* virtual training platform. This practice shows competence, expertise, and integrity, all of which help a customer trust you and buy from you and not your competitor.

Integrity: Know What You Stand For

If you don't stand for something, you'll fall for anything.

It's easy to say you won't bend the truth when times are good, when you don't need the money, or when you're on top of the pack, but how about when your spouse is sick or when the mortgage payment is overdue?

Decide what your values are. Know what you're willing to say or not say, no matter what's going on in your personal world. All aspects of your being must be in alignment for your message to resonate with the consumer.

Tell the Customer What Your Product Won't Do

When you only tell your customer the virtues of your product, you cease to be a reliable resource. One of the biggest complaints of customers today is that salespeople make the product sound "too good to be true."

This may seem counterintuitive, but if you don't share with a customer what is wrong, or what a product *won't* do, he'll never believe what it *will* do for him.

I put this idea to the test when selling my own car.

My dealer had offered me nowhere near Blue Book value, so I decided to take my chances and sell it on my own. Soon after posting my ad, a man came over to look at my car, a beautiful Land Rover that I'd priced fairly at $27,900—a couple thousand shy of Blue Book value. The first thing he wanted to know, naturally, was if the car had been in an accident. I answered him honestly.

"No," I said. "But let me tell you what is wrong with it."

He seemed stunned as I walked him around the car and pointed out some old problems that I had just repaired; they weren't things that he would have to worry about, because I had taken care of them, but I just felt that he would want to know. "The CD player is shot," I added. "You'll probably have to replace that whole thing."

He seemed clearly relieved. He thought he'd been in for some real bad news. It definitely made him stick around a little more to look at the car. Then he told me that the exact same model with *less* mileage on it was for sale in a neighboring town—for less money. I shrugged, eager to get back to my work. My partner and I had brochures spread all over the living room and I had a couple of other buyers coming to look at the car.

"Then you should buy the cheaper one," I said, meaning no more and no less than what I'd said.

"But yours is green," he said. "And I want a green car."

The other car wasn't precisely what he wanted. And because I had been so honest with him, he could see the value in getting just what he wanted, right when he wanted it. He also believed that it hadn't been in an accident because of how forthcoming I was about the drawbacks of the car (the dings, the repairs, and the broken CD player).

He gave me $1,000 to hold the car, and would return the next day to pay the balance. On his way out, he looked around the living room and asked what I did.

"I'm in sales," I answered, counting the money.

"Are you any good?"

I didn't have to answer, because my wonderful husband did it for me.

"Well, she just sold you a car, didn't she?"

The next day, he left with the car he wanted. I left the transaction with my ethics intact, and way more in my pocket than I would have if I had acted any other way. That day I learned, "If you're afraid to lose, you'll never win."

I didn't have a name for it at the time, but when I sold my car I used a technique I now call "baby negatives." A baby negative is a statement made to a customer, or an answer to a question, that reveals what your product *will not* do. Some things to remember:

* **Only use a baby negative** if the information you are offering is in fact a *baby* negative, not a giant negative.
* **When a customer asks a question, remember that questions can often be objections in disguise.** Clarify your customer's questions or concerns before answering with a baby negative or any other type of rebuttal.
* **Balance a "take-away" with an "add-on."** Remember the basic rule of a take-away: When you take something away, you must give something back. Tell your customer what your product *won't do*—but then follow up with what it *will do*.

Baby negatives are effective as long as your intent is pure. When adopting any sales technique, don't ever use it to control or manipulate. Do a gut check and ask yourself if your actions are meant to benefit your customer or if you're acting out of self-preservation. As Napoleon Hill wrote in *Think and Grow Rich*, "I fully realize that no wealth or position can long endure, unless built upon truth and justice, therefore, I will engage in no transaction that does not benefit all whom it affects."[5]

Go on an Integrity Cleanse

To have integrity with others, you must first practice integrity with yourself. What are your values? Do you keep your own commitments? This is tough. Lots of us are quick to cheat ourselves out of the things we need to be healthy and happy. Do you forego short-term pleasures for your long-term goals?

It's easier to sell with integrity when you practice it with yourself.

I listened to an amazing podcast the other day featuring bestselling author, Martha Beck. When asked how she does her very best work, she says she goes on an "integrity cleanse."[6] That is, she makes a commitment to tell the absolute truth on a deeper and deeper level. She says the more honest you are, the more magical you become, the easier life is, and the more successful you are.

What would an integrity cleanse look like to you? Be honest. Do you ever catch yourself telling white lies to make a social situation less awkward? Do you exaggerate project features when you're feeling nervous? Insights on integrity will come to you with practice. Ask yourself or ask a mentor, "What would you do if?" As Paul Samuelson says, "Good questions outrank easy answers."[7] Pay attention to the little things because when we slip on the small stuff, it has a way of snowballing into big stuff.

There's no guidebook on how a salesperson should behave. Let your conscience be your guide. Each of us must define for ourselves what values we hold and who we want to be. Trustworthiness is more than integrity. It's a rich, time-tested recipe made up of empathy, reliability, competency, and integrity.

This leads us to the next chapter, which is about caring deeply enough to ask the right questions. Doing so will help you find out what matters most to your customers and everyone else in your life.

CHAPTER 7

Anything That Can Be Told Can Be Asked

Universal Truth #7: When we ask the right questions, we uncover what matters most. "Discovery questions" uncover customers' needs, direct their thinking down a path we choose, generate curiosity, and ultimately move them to action. These questions build rapport, gain commitment, and help your prospects sell themselves. Well-crafted questions help us make a point loudly, without having to raise our voice. Good questions create change. Great questions can change the world.

Questions Help Us Fall in Love

I was fascinated with the *New York Times* article, "The 36 Questions That Lead to Love" which references Mandy Len Catron's *Modern Love* essay, "To Fall in Love With Anyone, Do This."

The idea is that 36 well-crafted, thought-provoking, emotional questions can cause you to fall in love with anyone. The questions are divided into three sections—each one more probing than the last. The thought is that mutual vulnerability fosters closeness. To quote the study's authors, "One key pattern associated with the development of a close relationship among peers is sustained, escalating, reciprocal, personal self-disclosure. Allowing oneself to be vulnerable with another person can be exceedingly difficult, so this exercise forces the issue."[1]

I was intrigued, so I decided to try it with my husband. After just 10 questions, we felt closer—more connected and happier. You can find the full list of questions at *www.nytimes.com/2015/01/11/fashion/no-37-big-wedding-or-small.html*, but here are a few:

* What would constitute a "perfect" day for you?
* If you were able to live to the age of 90 and retain either the mind or body of a 30-year-old for the last 60 years of your life, which would you want?
* If you could wake up tomorrow having gained any one quality or ability, what would it be?

Admittedly, I never tried this experiment with my hairdresser or a perfect stranger in an airplane. It was set up for those who already have an affinity for each other. But it still got me thinking: Why do questions help us build a heartfelt connection? And if 36 well-crafted questions can induce love, can 36 properly positioned questions lead to a sale?

Absolutely. Ask the right questions at the right time in the right way and the answers you receive will set you up for long-term success. This kind of methodological questioning, first proposed by Socrates some 2,400 years ago in classical Athens, has helped people and organizations clarify intentions, expand their thinking, and help opposing parties reach agreement ever since.

The great motivator Tony Robbins says that the human brain is a question-answering machine.[2] Ask lousy questions and you'll get lousy results. Ask better questions, you'll get better answers. The questions we ask our customers will dictate how they think about our products, about us, and about whether to buy right now.

This chapter is about knowing what questions to ask to uncover customer needs, to enjoy richer and more rewarding relationships, and to make more sales faster.

The Power of the Right Questions

Specifically, questions do several things. They:

* **Challenge our thinking and give birth to new ideas.** In life, we uncover thousands of possibilities, sometimes leading to new relationships, business opportunities, and novel ways of doing things. But we need that initial germ of an idea. Polaroid was founded on a single question from an engineer's 3-year-old: "Daddy, why do we have to wait to see our pictures?"
* **Create connection.** The word "communication" comes from the Latin word, *communis*, meaning "common." Questions help us connect through a commonality of values and ideas. As John Maxwell says, "Good questions prompt your customers to say 'me, too' instead of 'so what?'"[3]
* **Foster engagement.** When you're talking, you have no idea what your customer is thinking. For all you know, they're wondering, "When is she going to be quiet?" or, "I already knew that." Questions keep customers engaged.
* **Move a customer out of resistance.** The typical default response for salespeople when somebody keeps saying "no" is to keep selling the same idea. Instead, ask a question like, "Why do you say that?" or "Why do you feel it's too expensive?"
* **Move us to action.** Typically, statements trigger our brains' logical and analytical skills. Questions, on the other hand, trigger creative and emotional skills. Statements cause our prospects to think, and questions cause them to act.

The "No Asking" Price

Corey sells new homes for Strident Development Group. For the last 26 years, she has maintained the number-two or -three position in the company. Lately, however, she can't seem to make a sale.

Corey is confused. The developer just acquired fabulous new inventory. It seems like a perfect match for her customers. Finally, she can sell four-bedroom homes, not just studios. Not only that, the new development features a complete health club facility, day care, and an on-site restaurant. Corey believes in her product so much that she bought one for herself! So why won't her customers buy?

Corey suspects the customers probably prefer the west side of town, and that the maintenance fees for her new inventory are too high.

The truth is that Corey's lack of sales has nothing to do with her customers and everything to do with *her*.

I asked Corey and the rest of the team a few questions (how appropriate, right?), and the conversations revealed an unusual clue. Since their new product came on the scene, the sales team had consistently cut their presentation time nearly in half. As I dug deeper, it became apparent that nearly all of the seasoned sales force had reduced their presentation time by 38 percent.

Why?

It turned out that in their excitement to offer solutions, they had either shortened or eliminated their discovery step completely.

Neil Rackham, author of *Spin Selling*, uncovered the reason behind this phenomenon in his study of young Xerox salesmen. At Xerox, new salespeople hit the ground running—they were incredibly successful right out of the gates. Then, like clockwork, after 18 months, new reps crashed and burned.

What was Rackham's conclusion? Once sellers had become so-called experts, they started anticipating customer objections and offering generic solutions. Moreover, they were so excited about their offering that they stopped listening and started selling before uncovering individual buyer needs.[4] I see this happen all the time. New reps in their innocence and enthusiasm sell like crazy. Then, several months later, they get smart. They give too much information, overcome objections that weren't there in the first place, and ultimately lose the sale.

In his webinar "Why Salespeople Fail," Mike Bosworth (who worked with Rackham), created a term for this. He calls it "Premature Elaboration."[5] Are you a victim of Premature Elaboration Syndrome?

Many salespeople, like Corey, get so excited about their product that they assume everyone else will share their enthusiasm. They forget to ask the questions that will reveal their customers' true feelings. Eager to show their smarts and get the deal, they miss unique buying motives and signals.

Asking good questions in your discovery—and throughout the sales process—not only helps you uncover buyer needs, it helps you tailor the rest of your sales presentation to those needs.

Yesterday's salespeople merely needed to provide information. But today, buyers can find all the information they need online. So today's salespeople need to *interpret* that information, ask questions, and then spark an emotional need for their product. Few salespeople show the customer how they'll *feel* as a result of using their product or service, yet this emotional bond marks the difference between those salespeople, leaders, and companies that inspire, and those whose careers prematurely expire.

Exercise: Identify Your Discovery Questions

We can't make this emotional connection with random questions. In fact, asking the wrong questions at the wrong time can alienate your customers. You may have heard that there's no such thing as a stupid question? There are tons of stupid questions. Salespeople are notorious for asking irrelevant and unnecessary questions.

You will make far more sales by asking a series of targeted, thoughtful, and empathetic questions in your discovery than delivering a perfectly practiced presentation.

Jot down all of the questions you ask or think you should ask during this step of your sales process.

I find if you commit these questions to writing, you can't succumb to a psychological principle called *hindsight bias*. Hindsight bias occurs when we feel that we knew something all along. At my live seminars, if I lay out what questions to ask, salespeople often feel as though they're already asking them. However, when they commit their questions to writing first, they are often surprised at how many questions they're missing—and why it's costing them valuable sales.

Hold onto your list. You'll need it in a moment.

Travel the Most Direct Route: Find the Big Four

Can you imagine driving from one end of the country to the other without directions? You may eventually get to your destination, but without a map or GPS, you'll take far longer than necessary.

Your customers may not be as flexible. When your presentation is too long or off-point due to a lack of precision, your customers, to continue the analogy, may simply *run out of gas*. Your customers today are busy. They're overwhelmed. Side-road conversations that aren't relevant to them are simply an annoyance. You've got to keep them speeding down the interstate, not getting lost on side roads.

Your job is to ask questions so that you can provide solutions that are specific to their needs—the WIFM, or "What's in it for me?" Your questions must follow a logical order. In other words, you start by gathering facts, and then progress to deeper questions that uncover customers' problems and emotional motivators.

In the following section, I'll explain how to use my Third-Level selling methodology to craft a discovery that helps you uncover what I call the "Big Four." These are:

1. Get the facts about your customer's current situation with first- and second-level questions.
2. Discover the dominant buying motive with Third-Level questions.
3. Find the problem. Dig deep to determine the implications of the problem.
4. Uncover hidden objections or concerns.

What follows is the map you'll need for asking the right questions.

Third-Level Selling

Years ago, when I first started selling vacation ownership, I created levels of questions that helped me uncover my customers' emotional motivators. I called this methodology *Third-Level selling*. I began to help other salespeople in my office use Third-Level questions to connect with customers: I had discovered my niche.

I started to realize that if I could do this for individuals, I could do it for teams, and if I could do it for teams, I could help companies grow their revenues and transform their cultures.

This technique helps us get to the heart of the real reasons customers buy. The idea is to start with the facts and build up to those deeper questions so we can uncover buyer motivations:

* **First-level questions** uncover "facts."
* **Second-level questions** uncover "fact-feelings"—these bridging questions take us a little closer to the customer's core emotional motivators.
* **Third-Level questions** uncover the "emotional connection"— the deeper emotional reasons people buy.

Here's an example of Third-Level selling in action:

Salesperson's first-level (fact) question: Do you currently have a life insurance policy?

Prospect: No. We've never really felt the need for one.

[Is this answer enough for you to get the sale? It's probably not. Follow up with a bridging second-level question.]

Salesperson's second-level (fact-feeling) question: Are you thinking it might be a good idea now?

Prospect: Maybe. We have two young kids now.

[We're getting closer.]

Salesperson's Third-Level (emotional connection) question: *Why* would having a policy be important?

Prospect (*thinks for a moment*): If anything were to happen to me, my wife would have to go to work and the children would be left alone during the day. I couldn't put my family through that type of stress.

Salesperson: So having a policy in place would give you a great deal more security?

Prospect: Yeah, if it were affordable.

Bingo! What was the customer's Third-Level reason for purchasing? It was for security and family. The more emotional the response, the more urgency you will create.

Does Third-Level Selling Work in Business-To-Business (B2B)?

Businesses have a responsibility for their bottom line. They want to know how your solution will affect revenue, decrease turnover, and enhance customer satisfaction.

But remember: Individuals run organizations. They, too, have underlying emotional motivators that drive their decision-making—whether it's looking good to the boss, relieving stress, or building a more fulfilling work environment. *People, not institutions, make decisions.*

With that in mind, remember that when selling to businesses, these motivators may be hidden under the surface. It's your job to uncover them and show how they're connected to metrics like revenue, retention, and reputation.

Here's an example of Third-Level selling in a business-to-business (B2B) context:

Salesperson's first-level (fact) question: How long is your current contract with your copier supplier?

Prospect: Oh, we're in it for another 12–18 months, I believe.

Salesperson's second-level (fact-feeling) question: Are you happy with your service?

Prospect: It seems fine.

[At this point, the novice salesperson would jump straight to price savings. But the Third-Level seller was really listening.]

Salesperson: You say "*seems* fine." If you could change anything, what would it be?

Prospect: Well, we have to physically take the copiers across town for servicing.

Salesperson's Third-Level (emotional connection) question: How does that affect you personally?

Prospect (*thinks for a moment*): The employees hate having to leave the store for half a day and the customers often have to wait for their product. It slows down production.

Salesperson: What does the downtime cost you?

Prospect: It's hard to say, but it's not ideal.

Salesperson: So, in addition to saving you money on downtime, having on-site servicing would improve morale and customer service?

Prospect: Yeah, I guess so.

Salesperson: What a significant contribution that would be in your first year!

Prospect: How much is it?

Remember Why Prospects Buy

When it comes to selling, the heart always comes before the head. If you're on a team that inspires you, or you've followed a boss who's motivated you, you know that that leader didn't merely tell you how to do something; she *inspired* you to do it. It came from within. You were emotional about your commitment. So whether you're selling dance lessons, real estate, software, or life insurance, people buy on emotion and justify their decisions with logic *after the fact.*

To refresh your memory, here are the seven key emotional drivers for all human behavior that we distinguished in Chapter 2. This time, I've also included the fear associated with the absence of each motivator.

Avoid the Anvil

When it comes to motivation, all decisions are an attempt to move toward pleasure or away from pain.[6] But remember that the urge to avoid immediate pain is more stirring than our desire for pleasure. Wile E. Coyote, in the Roadrunner cartoons, moved more slowly to find food than he did to avoid the anvil dropping on his head.

Hope for gain	Fear of loss
Safety	Death
Adventure	Boredom
Significance	Insignificance, no legacy
Relationships	Loneliness
Health and wellness	Sickness
Sense of purpose	Confusion, despair
Growth and education	Ignorance

Here's the fun part: Remember when I asked you to write down the questions you typically ask in your discovery? Take a look at your list. Knowing that people buy for Third-Level or emotional reasons, ask yourself, "Am I asking enough Third-Level questions?" Are you asking any?

If customers are buying for the Third-Level reasons, why aren't you asking Third-Level questions?

Craft Questions to Increase Market Share

If you've discovered that you weren't asking enough Third-Level questions, you're not alone. Most salespeople don't. For example, Justin is in charge of the enterprise sales division for a major retailer selling franchises to entrepreneurs around the globe at $200,000 a pop. His company—let's call it "SunnyFish"—retains a large share of the profits.

Justin is charming, charismatic, and full of energy. He told me sales were good, but could be better.

"Show me your discovery questions," I asked.

He was quiet.

"Well I don't really have any written down," he admitted. "I go with my gut."

We did a little role-playing, and as it turns out, the majority of his questions were first level:

1. Have you ever owned a business?
2. How's your credit score?
3. Who would you employ to help you?

"Okay," I said. "Those questions are great *qualifying* questions, but they'll do nothing to get your customers to *want* to buy a franchise. You need to find out what makes them tick. Well-crafted Third-Level questions create a need for your product that was never there in the first place."

At first, Justin seemed puzzled. But he seemed open to my suggestion, so I went on and explained the three levels of questions to him. Together, we crafted a list of Third-Level questions:

1. Why do you want to be in business for yourself?
2. What would being your own boss mean to you?
3. Why would that be important?

What happened next was nothing short of miraculous. Potential customers were no longer just methodically going through the motions and responding to qualifying questions. Justin's questions opened their hearts to new possibilities. The questions themselves stirred something deep inside of them and moved them to action.

"There is no shortcut to winning sales," I told Justin. "You must prepare the tough questions and practice them in advance."

The secret to getting level three responses is to tread slowly at first. Ask fact-finding first-level questions before moving to the more useful Third-Level questions. You know you're moving to the Third Level when the response you hear hits one of the seven key motivators—or their associated fears. You know you've gotten here when you can feel a demonstrable shift in the emotional state of your customer.

Justin phoned me the next month. Sales are up by 42 percent!

Go Deep: Craft Third-Level Questions

Top performers ask questions that are so precise they prompt customers to view their businesses or their lives differently.

1. **Ask why:** When you ask "who, what, when, and where" questions, you will often get a first-level response. "Why" questions, on the other hand, usually move the customer to level three.

2. **Tell me more:** The more you listen, the more your customers will share. Use phrases such as "Tell me more," and "Then what happened?" Make sure to smile and nod (unless you sell cemetery plots or burials at sea).

3. **Uncover life priorities:** We also need to be asking the big "What" question: "What is the most important thing in your life?" Rather than asking this question directly, you can start by asking the customer how they might prioritize your product offering. For example:

   * How important is buying a second home to you, on a scale of 1–10?
   * How important is financial freedom to you, on a scale of 1–10?
   * How important is finding the right supplier to you, on a scale of 1–10?

   Let's say they answer a one—or even a four. Many salespeople give up at this point. They figure their customers aren't that interested. They miss the whole point. Well-crafted Third-Level questions reveal interest when there appears at first blush to be none.

Savvy salespeople follow up this response with the question, "What's a 10?" When you sell with heart, you uncover your customers' core motivators and link your product to them. This is what results in true urgency.

PUT IT INTO PRACTICE
UNCOVER "THE BIG FOUR"

1. **Get the facts about your customer's current situation with first- and second-level questions.**

   Goal: *Ask questions that reveal the customer's current situation or the status quo.*

Business-to-Consumer First-Level Questions

1. Have you used this type of program before?
2. What/who do you use now?
3. Do you like it?
4. How often do you use it?
5. How many times have you [fill in the blanks]?

Business-to-Business First-Level Questions

1. How long have you worked for your company?
2. What platform do you use now?
3. What accountability systems do you have in place to measure and monitor performance? What else do you measure? Why?
4. How many employees do you have? How much turnover do you have?
5. Is your team moving through their pipeline effectively?

You get the picture.

Second-level questions are a follow-up to your first question. They acknowledge the facts that your customer has just shared. Most importantly, second-level questions act as a bridge to the more powerful Third-Level questions.

2. **Discover dominant buying motives with Third-Level questions.**

Goal: Ask questions that reveal the emotional or Third-Level reasons they'll buy—their hopes and fears.

Examples of Third-Level Questions

1. Why are you interested in this model?
2. Why now? Why are you interested in engagement software for your employees?
3. What's important to you in a vacation?
4. Is there still something you would like to accomplish?
5. Why would having an insurance plan be important to you?
6. Why do you want to redecorate your home?
7. What would you do with the extra money?
8. Why did you take that new position?
9. How does this problem affect you personally?
10. What do you feel you need to accomplish in your tenure here?

3. **Find the problem and dig deep to determine the implications of the problem.**

Goal: Find a problem that your product will solve. But don't stop there—make customers understand the deeper implications of that problem.

Common problems your questions are likely to unearth:

* Not enough time.
* Poor customer service.
* Poor quality.
* Difficult to use.
* Too slow.
* Too expensive.

The following questions can help you uncover these problems:

* Are you looking for a quick fix or are you seeking lasting results?
* If you could change anything, what would it be?
* What's your worst experience with. . . ?
* Has it always been that way? (Get the prospect to think about how he felt *before* the problem occurred.)
* What will happen if you do nothing?
* How big is the problem, on a scale of 1–10?
* Whose neck will be on the chopping block if this problem doesn't go away?
* Are you committed to change?
* Why now?

Of course, finding a problem isn't always enough to move the customer from the status quo. You also need to reveal the larger implications of that problem. You want to make it clear the implications of the problem are so tangible that she'll pay any price to make it go away, if that is indeed the case.

For example, just the other day, a faucet was leaking in the master bathroom in our home. I was busy and wanted to ignore it. But my husband pointed out that if we didn't call a plumber, we risked ruining our wood floors. What was the impact of this problem? Oh, about $10,000. I phoned the plumber and happily paid him the $650 to fix the faucet. It wasn't enough for me to know there was a problem; I had to see clearly the consequences of failing to solve it. The more severe and costly the problem, the more urgently your customer will want to solve it.

One of my favorite slogans is "Sooner or later, you'll break down and call AAA." The implication is that the cost of an AAA membership is miniscule compared with the cost of being stuck on the side of the road with smoke pouring out of your engine and no one to call.

Similarly, Fram Oil Filter used to have ads that said, "You can pay me now or pay me later." Again, it's not just the problem that's highlighted, *it's the cost of not solving the problem right now.* Keep asking why the situation is a problem, why the prospect can't solve it themselves, and what will happen if they don't. More sales than you may think are lost when salespeople don't internalize—and act on—this concept.

4. **Uncover hidden objections or concerns.**

   Goal: *Even your best customers will have some concerns holding them back from pulling the trigger. Ask questions to help you identify and address these hidden objections.*

   Our office gets more requests for seminars that deal with closing and handling objections than all of our other courses combined. What's the problem? Overcoming objections at the back end isn't nearly as productive as uncovering them at the front end. If you have a craving for fish tacos, I need to know that before I build a menu around bison burgers.

   You know the expression "no questions, no objections, no sale"? It's your job to uncover all possible objections and concerns *before* you ask for the order. You can get a "no" now or get one later. Best to get it now while you still have time to clarify it and overcome it. Discovery objections are usually pre-conceived objections. Newer objections may appear throughout the sales call and you must determine their validity and overcome them as they surface.

COMMON OBJECTIONS

- I can buy it cheaper or get better value elsewhere.
- I don't need it.
- I don't believe it/I don't believe you.
- I can't afford it.
- It's too complicated—too much effort.

The following questions will help you better uncover objections:

1. Have you ever considered purchasing this type of product before? Why did or didn't you buy it?
2. What's changed?
3. Who else have you contacted for this type of product? What do you like about their offering?
4. What would your friends, boss, or family say if you purchased this?
5. What are the biggest challenges to implementing this, buying this, owning this?

How to Ask Good Questions

How you ask is just as important as what you ask. Salespeople often memorize thought-provoking questions, but deliver them in an off-putting way. Buyers recoil when you go too deep, too fast. They resent it when you ask them to fill out a checklist of predetermined questions without taking a personal interest in each response. They feel manipulated when you fire back solutions before delving deeper into their feelings and problems.

Conversely, when you are generally curious and thoughtful—and even ask surprising questions—your prospects will respect you and connect with you. Periodically repeat back what you've heard, and your prospects will be amazed. I've actually had customers tell me, "This is the best product I've seen yet!" before I'd gotten around to showing them anything. I'd simply listened and repeated back what they told me they liked, didn't like, and were pumped up about.

Because how you ask is just as important as what you ask, I've created a comprehensive list of action steps for crafting good questions in your discovery and beyond.

1. **Move from the general to the specific.**

    I like to start my discovery with a very general question like, "Tell me about yourself and your company" or "Tell me about you and your training programs."

Pay attention to whether they answer your question or tell you something else entirely. (They may tell you, "We're just looking," or, "We're not happy with the service we get from your company," for example.) Their response will clue you in to what's foremost on their minds and in their hearts.

2. **Let the customer finish her train of thought.**

Have you heard the saying, "He who speaks first after a closing question loses"? Well, you have now! The same holds true during your discovery. Customers are more likely to be vulnerable when you give them some space. I find that salespeople often can't stand the pressure of a moment of silence, so they rush to fill the void. Be curious enough to see what the customer says. What you think is "end of communication" may just be a long, thoughtful pause.

3. **Compliment, don't criticize.**

Don't put your customers on the defensive or they will react by shutting down. I often hear misguided salespeople insult their customers' choices with comments like:

* That learning software package you use isn't open-source, so it's inferior to our proprietary learning software.
* You camp every year? Yuck. You should consider upgrading your travel.

Last year, my family and I traveled to a fly fishing lodge in Alaska. A guest once said to Max, the owner, "You must have non-stop headaches, being responsible for this place," and Max moved into full-on defense mode: "I get paid for fishing and flying a float plane. I love it!" Two days later, another guest said his dream was to own a fishing lodge, and Max confessed, "It's non-stop, fixing the heaters, training the guides, and installing new gas pumps!" As a general rule, when you tell someone what's wrong with a product choice or idea, they'll tell you what's right about it. When you compliment their choices, chances are better they'll reveal the problems.

4. **Stay with your customer.**

Too many salespeople hand their customer's surveys and walk away, or send them discovery questions online. Your customer will give you more complete and in-depth answers when you stay with them through the discovery process. Every time I'm asked to fill out a survey at the doctor's office, I give the shortest possible answers and skip what I can get away with. Your customers are no different.

5. **Flying on autopilot during your discovery is not an option.**

Write out all of your questions to ensure that each question is intentional and yields one of the Big Four types of answers I described earlier in this chapter. If you already have prescribed discovery questions, make sure each question fits into one of the four categories.

6. **Get the rest of the story.**

In Chapter 5, I offered techniques to build rapport when you seemingly share little in common. Follow-up questions in the discovery step not only build greater rapport, they also unlock critical information.

Ask questions, listen to the answers, and use the answers to ask the next meaningful question. Prospects will generally answer the questions you ask them, no more and no less.

When you ask a question, dig deeper and ask follow-up questions to get the rest of the story. I love to illustrate this point in seminars with a clip from the movie *The Return of the Pink Panther*.

The scene begins with Inspector Clouseau checking into a German hotel. He sees a small dog sitting next to the hotelier, and as he reaches down to pet it, asks, "Does your dog bite?"

The hotelier answers, "No."

Clouseau proceeds to pat the small dog's head until the dog snaps and ferociously bites him.

"I thought you said your dog didn't bite!" Clouseau cries.

The hotelier replies: "That is not my dog."

What's Next?

Now that you've uncovered the Big Four, what do you do with that information? Well, for starters, we need to make certain that the information we received is in fact what our customer meant to tell us. Top performers not only uncover essential information, they confirm it.

Uncovering and confirming your customer's life priorities and challenges is a start. But you can't change someone's priorities with a dynamic sales presentation. You can't *make* your technology or your medicine or your car or your financial plan the most compelling thing in your customer's life. What you *can* do is find out what your customer's life priorities are and link your product to it.

This practice creates urgency—the need to buy *right this minute.* Wouldn't you like your customers not just to buy, but to feel an urgent need to? How to get them to feel just that is the subject of the next chapter.

CHAPTER 8

Emotional Commitment Precedes Economic Commitment

Universal Truth #8: Most salespeople incorrectly assume that they can create a sense of urgency by threatening scarcity or appealing to greed. But if people don't want what you're selling, they won't care if there are only two left or what else you're throwing in. (Anyone want a stagecoach? It's on sale today only! And I'll throw in some horseshoes for free!) In this chapter, I'll discuss ways to engage customers with stories and build urgency by demonstrating how your product connects to precisely what motivates them.

The Magical Elevator

Decades ago, when operators still manned elevators all around New York City, a small crowd hovered outside the entrance to the 181st subway station, jockeying for space on Bruce Renfroe's elevator to the tracks below.[1] At first, Bruce's elevator seemed like any other in Manhattan. It was stinking of grease, with gum-covered floors and a claustrophobic, coffinesque feeling of confinement. But Bruce took that airless box and made his ride an experience for his "customers" to look forward to.

One day, Bruce pinned up a magazine picture of dishes because he liked the pattern. It got a fair amount of attention, and shortly after, a customer brought in a picture of a thoroughbred horse. Others followed suit until the elevator walls were practically wallpapered with bright pictures of everything from golf clubs to cruise ships to guitars. Bruce brought in a vase of fresh flowers and placed them in the corner. He loved the cool sound of jazz music, so he hooked up his cassette player to a tiny speaker and began to broadcast Louis Armstrong and Duke Ellington, smooth and mellow.

Only one thing was missing. He placed a bin in the rear corner and dropped a couple of cans of tomato soup in it. "What's that for?" asked a passenger.

"It's for those in need," replied Bruce, smiling.

Passengers added Cheerios, noodles, and canned beans. Bruce collected up to a thousand pounds of food every month.

You can imagine what happened next. There came a rainy afternoon when Bruce arrived for the late shift and discovered his elevator had been stripped. Not a single picture or plant—and worse, no bin for the needy. A bigwig from City Hall had heard about Bruce's elevator: All those decorations were against regulations. When the passengers rushed from the train to his elevator, they were dismayed. "Where's all of the stuff?"

Bruce explained about the city policy, and when he opened the doors a few passengers got off, but most stayed right where they were. "Bruce, take us back down with you, so we can talk to the head honcho."

They stepped out of the elevator and surrounded the president of the New York City Transit Authority, telling him that riding in Bruce's elevator was the highlight of their day. They didn't want to see a thing change. The president gave in. By the end of the shift, everything was right back where it belonged.

What was happening in that three-minute elevator ride? How was Bruce able to shift these people's entire day in just three minutes? Whatever it was, it made busy New Yorkers take time out of their day to defend a relative stranger, to care deeply about something that—for everyone else in the city—was of zero consequence. New Yorkers are notorious for avoiding personal interaction. They bury their heads in newspapers, drown out voices with ear buds, and snarl at anyone who dares to make eye contact. (As a comedian once joked, "In the New York subways, making eye contact is giving the other person permission to kill you.")

Does that sound like any of your customers lately? So what's the formula from moving someone from suspicion and disengagement to warmth, receptivity, and engagement? In other words, what can we learn from Bruce?

Bruce fulfilled a basic human need; he brought a sense of community to disconnected strangers. He showed how you could create a lot with a little. But I believe he did something much more vital. In an instant, he shifted the emotional state of his passengers. He created an emotional experience that made them feel good and caused them to take an immediate action. You can learn to do exactly the same thing.

Why is affecting the emotional state of the customer so important? *Because emotions cause people to act.* A sales presentation that generates a deep, memorable, emotional experience—coupled with a product that fulfills your customers' wants and needs—results in a phenomenon I call *emotional urgency.*

Get Your Prospect's Permission

If you've been in sales for longer than a minute, you have probably been taught to create urgency in one of the following ways:

* Make it clear that your offer expires.
* Offer extras that are contingent on buying now.
* Threaten a price increase or a loss of incentives.

Let me ask you a question. Despite your best efforts at creating urgency, are you still hearing replies like "I need to think about it," "We need to check our budget," or "The timing just isn't right"?

If you're like most salespeople I talk to, the answer is "yes."

I've got news for you. No one cares if there's only two left or the price goes up next week if they don't want or need what you are selling in the first place. You can't hijack your customers' minds and force your incentives upon them.

You can't create urgency without a prospect's permission. But people will give you permission if they are emotionally committed to what you are selling. When you align what you're selling with what they're feeling, they will open their hearts and their wallets.

Master the Three Components of Emotional Urgency

Emotional urgency influences human behavior. Understand how to create it and you will win bigger deals, create more profound relationships, and build deeper trust.

At this point, you've built trust in the warm-up phase, made your agenda clear, and performed an in-depth Third-Level discovery. If you've done this correctly, you haven't begun to sell or solve anything yet. What you *have* done is gathered the information you need to create a compelling emotional sales experience that leads to an action *today*.

Now you've reached the product presentation phase of your sales process, the time for putting all of that information to good use. I've seen countless salespeople ask poignant discovery questions only to deliver a generic sales presentation. At this point, your customers want to know one thing: What's in it for me (WIFM)? They want to know you can fulfill their desires and solve their problems. But before you can link their needs with your offer and make a compelling case for your product, you must confirm that you got the information right.

In other words, no matter what you're selling, or whom you're selling to, you must complete each of these three steps in order to build that vital sense of emotional urgency.

* Confirm your customer's wants, needs, and concerns.
* Link their wants and needs to your product.
* Create an emotional experience through evocative stories and a memorable sales experience.

Create a Feedback Loop

If you've ever been rock climbing, you're familiar with these commands:

"On belay!"

"Climbing!"

"Climb on!"

These are the life-and-death verbal signals used by rock climbers to confirm that both parties understand where they are, where they're headed, and that it's time to move forward. Many fatal accidents have resulted from a break in this feedback loop.

Creating a feedback loop is essential for salespeople, too. Why? Although simple facts—like the spelling of a name—are easy to check and correct, it's much trickier to listen and articulate back how your customer *feels*.

Salespeople often assume they've discovered the accurate information, but they miss or misinterpret critical facts. And we all know what happens when we assume.

Recently, I spoke to an old friend who had lost her husband to cancer four years earlier. She told me she'd been spending a lot of time with Bob, her accountant, and that he didn't think she should live alone any more.

I excitedly confirmed back to her, "So there's a spark between you and Bob, huh?"

"Oh no," she laughed. "He's my son's age. He thinks I need to move into a senior living facility!"

It's a good thing I used a confirmation statement, or I'd be planning a wedding! How often do you project your thoughts, ideas, hopes, and fears onto your customers? It probably happens more often than you think.

Depending on your sales process, you can either launch into a confirmation statement directly after your discovery or at the beginning of a follow-up meeting. Information confirmation is, simply, the act of repeating back the information you heard and getting confirmation that what you heard is, in fact, what the customer meant.

This step ensures that you get the whole truth. In longer sales cycles, it allows you to control the agenda and prevent changes from having an impact on your sales process.

According to Ken Ferry, founder of the Korn Ferry Institute,

This kind of listening is difficult to master, in part because it is at odds with today's frenetically-multitasking, information-overloaded, distraction-driven world but, perhaps more importantly, because it runs counter to the way our brains have evolved to function. Our listening brain is wired to do exactly what active listening discourages: evaluate input, predict outcomes, make judgments, and perform triage, all on a moment-to-moment basis.[2]

Recently, I made the costly and embarrassing error of omitting this step. David, the VP of sales and decision-maker at his company, had sought me out to create a custom online curriculum for his inside sales department team. David was excited. After three separate meetings (including an in-depth discovery) we met for the fourth time, intent on discussing the project's scope and financial terms.

When I sat down for the meeting, two new people sat down: the new curriculum designer, as well as David's new boss. After a few niceties, David's boss looked at me and asked, "So, what are you trying to sell us?"

I was taken aback. I wasn't prepared to tout my bio and qualifications. After all, David had clearly been trying to sell *me*. He was trying to get me to fit him into my overly booked schedule—or so I had thought. Had I either started the meeting with a verbal confirmation statement or, better yet, delivered a written agenda confirming the status of the discussions, I would have had a much better shot at moving the initiative forward.

PUT IT INTO ACTION

Information Confirmation How-To's

1. **Repeat back the first-level information you uncovered in the discovery.**

    Repeat back names, dates, trigger events, and places, and you will increase trust in the process. With consumers, focus more on personal information, like family and activities. For businesses, shift your attention to current suppliers, chains of command, and roles and responsibilities within the company.

Susan, a leadership consultant for a large firm in the Colorado area, has mastered information confirmation. After meeting the CEO of one of the fastest-growing medical out-sourcing companies for the third time and performing several in-depth discoveries, she confirmed the first-level information to the CEO this way:

> *Let me see if I understand this correctly: You just started your company* On Site Medical *two years ago, in May. In fact, OSM just celebrated its two-year anniversary at La Mademoiselle res-taurant last week. You've experienced phenomenal growth—from five employees to more than 500—and you're the premier pro-vider of on-site medical care in the state.*
>
> *Your goal is to expand your services to Phoenix and California. You have a new executive, Warner, whom you just hired as vice president of sales and marketing—so that's been extremely help-ful. However, he's still a little bit green and has a lot to learn. Do I have that right so far?*

2. **Repeat the customer's Third-Level information.**

Repeating back the facts is a start. Next, you want to repeat back the customer's deeper Third-Level information. Confirm how the facts make the customer feel, and how those feelings might cause them to act:

> *You feel absolutely passionate about the work you've done as an internist for the last 15 years, but you feel there's been a real decline in the medical care available to the public, specifically, the care available to workers. Providing services on-site infinitely changes the health care experience. This goal consumes you and is on your heart and soul.*

Phew! How could the CEO resist? The consultant has just listened and repeated back what's in the CEO's heart and soul, what drives her, and what makes her life worth living. Talk about creating a sense of urgency to buy! As they say on the infomercials, however, "But wait! There's more!" And here it is: The key step missed by most salespeople.

3. **Repeat back the problem.**

   I realize the word "problem" can be confusing, so let me clarify. A problem is not an objection; it is the actual challenge your customer currently faces that your product will solve. Repeating back the customer's problem and the *implications* of that problem gives you implicit permission to solve it:

   With all of your success has come increased growth, which, while exciting, is creating leadership challenges. Currently your new executive team does not have clear roles, responsibilities, and systems of accountability. Obviously, this isn't your fault, but you do need to address it if you want to continue your aggressive growth plans. In fact, your plans for the new year call for 35-percent top line growth.

   Without a cohesive structure, this could have a serious impact on your profits as well as your brand. You've spoken to other consultants, but you didn't feel chemistry with them or feel that they took the time to really understand your organization's needs.

   After each of these steps, you want to make certain you're gaining agreement. Look for signs like:
   * Nodding in agreement.
   * Forward-leaning body language.
   * A verbal confirmation.

   All of this indicates—you guessed it—mounting urgency.

4. **Gain agreement.**

   Now that you've done the heavy lifting, ask your customer to confirm the information that you've repeated. While doing so, propose your solution. That solution should hit their dominant buying motive (DBM), solve their problems, and overcome their objections. It might go something like:

So, what you would be looking for in a consultant is some-one who shares your passion for health and wellness, someone who knows your industry, someone who will take the time and energy to get to know each of your executive team members on a personal level, and someone who has the ability to create a cohesive struc-ture and strategy to help you facilitate your growth, now and into the future. Is that about right or did I leave anything out?

You know you've performed a rock solid confirmation statement when the customer exclaims, "Wow, you really lis-tened!" or "You've got it, but there's one more thing I'd like to add. . . . "

Watch out for:

* Generic confirmation statements; they show that you weren't listening or you don't really care.
* Salespeople who don't pause and check for verbal and nonver-bal cues.
* Salespeople who project their thoughts and feelings on the customer rather than repeating back what they actually said.

Honing your confirmation skills makes a big difference in your performance. Once I got my confirmation statement down pat, I was amazed at how much more efficient my sales process became.

Expand Your Market Share

Mark was in trouble. His leads were awful; in fact, his customer base seemed to have dried up completely. As a franchisee of a direct furniture sales and refurbishment business, he remembered the days when it seemed like every-one was in renovation mode. He used to meet plenty of qualified customers at home shows—all of them excited about the idea of remodeling and ready to spend.

These days, most of his prospects were qualified only by their income. Not many of them actually wanted to buy.

"Since the recession," Mark lamented, "fewer consumers are remodeling. They have zero interest in refurbishing their homes. Closing percentages have plummeted to 10 percent."

"Refurbishing probably isn't a priority for them yet," I said, and then I asked Mark a simple question: "Do you agree that only 10 percent of the people in your area wake up in the morning thinking about refurbishing their homes?"

"That's probably about right," said Mark.

"*That's* why you're only closing 10 percent," I said. Then I asked him, "So what do 90 or 100 percent of the people in any area wake up thinking about, wanting, needing?"

Mark was silent.

"What do *you* want more of in your life?" I asked.

Mark thought a moment. "Less time working," he said. "And, of course, more time with my children, but they've gone to college and rarely visit."

I proposed a solution. "If you invested in a new family room, complete with a big-screen TV—perhaps an outdoor BBQ, a hydrotherapy spa, over-stuffed sofa, and fun room—might they come home for Christmas instead of staying at the dorm?" I went on, "Our neighbors down the street, the Conways, invested in a game room, horseshoe pit, and outdoor bar stocked to the gills! Now, instead of going to their friends' houses over college break, the kids can't wait to invite their friends over to visit at their cool parents' house."

I think I got him with the overstuffed sofa.

Weeks later, when I spoke to Mark, he told me about a couple who came in to browse. After a few minutes of asking the right questions, he found out that their daughter was getting married and moving into a new townhome with a dated kitchen. Within 30 minutes, the couple was signing paperwork for a furniture package for her wedding gift.

After we taught these Third-Level selling techniques to Mark's entire team, overall closing percentages increased by more than 35 percent. The next year of sales was far better than projected, allowing them to capture the market share they had been losing.

Too many salespeople think of themselves as simply order takers. If the customer isn't actively shopping for their product, rather than linking their priorities to their product, they give up and skip to another prospect. Top sellers, on the other hand, have learned to uncover the customer's hidden emotional (or business) needs, solve their problems, and *link* their product to that solution.

When you do this, you expand your market share to anyone and everyone seeking the benefits you're selling. You also get them to want to buy *right now*.

As you begin to ask the right questions and listen wholeheartedly, you create emotional urgency and your sales will increase dramatically. With practice, you will become better and better at asking the right questions, digging out what matters most to people, and prioritizing the customers' needs.

You're probably wondering, though, "What do I do with that information?" As Abraham Lincoln once said, "The man who doesn't read good books has no advantage over the man who can't read them." If you don't use the information you've discovered, you'll have no advantage over the salesperson that never uncovered the information in the first place!

What it all comes down to is this:

* **Good** salespeople do a discovery.
* **Better** salespeople ask the right questions in the discovery to uncover the Big Four: first-level facts, dominant buying motive (DBM), problems, and objections.
* **The Best** salespeople actually take the information from the discovery and *link* it emotionally to the features and benefits of their product, and then gain comittment.

Here's the basic formula:

1. **Give the customer a point of reference,** such as, "Earlier you were telling me is that as you look for bids from various staffing

companies, knowledge of your industry will be a key factor in your decision-making process."

2. **Select a feature of your product.** "The nice thing about Hardy staffing is that we have experts in over 40 different verticals, with 23 in banking alone."

3. **Point out your advantage.** "Most of our competitors simply provide staffing. We make it our business to understand your business."

4. **State the benefit to them.** "What this means to you is that we will bring you the best employees for your key positions and ensure you reduce the 36-percent turnover you're currently experiencing." Show what's in it for them by referring to their DBM, problem, or objection.

5. **End with a confirmation question.** "Is this the kind of specialization you're looking for?"

PUT IT INTO ACTION

Link or Sink

Let's take a closer look at defining features, advantages, and benefits.

* **Features:** Simply put, a feature is what your product does. It is a characteristic that is quantifiable and indisputable. Features alone won't motivate your prospects. It's the benefit of those features that elicit the decision to buy.

* **Advantages:** Advantages create a superiority of position. They're what sets your product offering apart from the competition and lets the prospect know why they should be doing business with your company and not someone else.

* **Benefits:** By definition, a benefit is something of value or usefulness. A benefit explains what the features mean to your

prospects—the problems they can solve and pleasures they can bring.

If you're selling new homes, a feature might be the home's recreation center. Its benefit is that it will help the homeowner stay healthy and fit. Here's how the linking part of your presentation might sound. Start with some point-of-reference based on what you already discussed:

Point of reference: *Earlier, you were telling me that one of your priorities is wellness and working out.*

Feature and advantage: *The nice thing about our development is that, unlike any other facility on this side of town, we have a 45,000-foot gym and spa.*

Benefit: *So you can maintain your regime of daily workouts without having to even get in your car!*

Confirmation question: *How does that sound?*

The confirmation question will yield either agreement or an objection. As I've noted elsewhere, it's better to get an objection now rather than later.

Here's an example of how someone selling learning software might approach this step:

Point of reference: *Earlier you were telling me you didn't have any systems of accountability to make certain your reps were retaining training concepts.*

Feature and advantage: *The benefit of our learning software is that we have leveraged some of the most sophisticated testing, monitoring, and reporting systems in the industry.*

Benefit: *You can test your sales reps' competency in everything from product knowledge to closing skills and determine which reps need additional training. By using this system of accountability, many of our clients increase production by more than 35 percent.*

Confirmation question:
Is that about right?

Anything else you'd like to add?
Do I have a good understanding of how you feel?

Linking Tips

1. **Link like a mountaineer.**

   Focus on your product's select features, advantages, and benefits that will be the most meaningful to the customer in front of you. Think of limiting benefits like packing for a mountaineering adventure. My family loves to go rock climbing and hiking. We've learned that, on an overnight journey, you must be sensible about what you pack. Everything you bring, you have to carry. Unnecessary items add weight. (If you saw the movie *Wild* you know exactly what I mean!) Excessive linking also adds weight and trips up your customer's buying process. Spotlight the three or four features and benefits that are most relevant.

   Remember: Too much information results in indecision.

2. **Don't use exact phrasing.**

   You don't have to regurgitate the formula exactly. In fact, if you do, it'll come across as cheesy. Remember: The purpose of the linking formula is to trigger your brain to link customer needs with product benefits. Vary the words without losing the impact.

3. **Get commitments.**

   Top salespeople gain commitment throughout their entire sales presentation. Although the linking formula ensures you're uncovering the WIFM, following it up with a commitment question increases urgency. Ask questions like:

   * "Does what I am proposing to you today meet all of your needs?"
     * There are two answers to that: yes or no. If the answer is "no," then ask, "What do I need to show you, or cover to make our product a match?"

- ✳ "Is ours the best solution?"
  - ✳ Here, again, there are only two answers. If it's "no," then ask "What do we need to do to make this the best solution for you?"

Asking these two questions will ensure, number one, that you really understand the buyers' needs, but more importantly, that your deal really addresses those needs. In a competitive situation, that second part tells you where you stand.

Depending on your product, you may ask other targeted questions about financing, timing, or decision-makers. Ask with confidence—get out on the skinny branches.

Stock Up on Stories

Many years ago, as my colleague Marta and I sat down to a large Christmas Eve buffet brunch, a couple of seniors—they *had* to be over 90 years old—marched in wearing red Santa hats with bells ringing in the tips. They were adorable. They sat down next to us, each of them with ear-to-ear grins. I couldn't help myself, so I leaned over and asked, "What's the secret to a happy marriage?"

The husband leaned toward me and said, "You know, I first met Helen out of the Navy. You may not know it now"—sitting taller—"but I was a handsome fellow back then. Helen kept pestering me to get married. I kept telling her, 'I need to think about it.'

"That's when she said, 'You'll never know how good it can be until you do it. Why not think about it while we're married?'

"And so I did. 67 years later, I'm still thinking about it!" They both giggled. They giggled their way through their ham, eggs, and cheesecake— happy and in love, all those years later.

Our brains love stories, but our hearts cherish them even more. For years, I told this story to couples who, at the moment of truth, just couldn't make a decision. It almost always pushed them over the edge.

New research confirms that hearing the right stories at the right time cause the brain to release oxytocin, the neurochemical responsible for empathy. Oxytocin, dubbed the "Moral Molecule," by neuroeconomist Paul Zak, makes people more trustworthy, generous, charitable, and compassionate![3] Researchers experimented on customers in a sales environment, having them ingest oxytocin through their nasal cavity to see if they would become more trusting and empathetic. (I figure if you can get a complete stranger to sniff an unknown chemical, he probably trusts you already!)

Even if your prospect is interested in the facts of your offering, he won't be inspired to act without his emotions leading the charge. Your customer may *think* your solution is right in his head, but he'll only take action when it feels right in his heart.

I'll Have What She's Having

Since the advent of social media, the way we promote our products and services has changed dramatically. We're living in a world of "I'll have what you're having." The thinking is that because you like it and I like *you*, it must be good for me. If you and I are virtual friends, you are 27 percent more likely to find credibility in a product recommended by me than by a pop-up, TV ad, billboard, or centerfold. In addition to creating an emotional experience, stories that involve other customers using and benefiting from your product add credibility to your offering.[4]

One of our clients, Jack, uses stories and anecdotes to describe almost every feature, advantage, and benefit of his product: "American Express found that 25 percent of their sales reps found this feature useful" or "JP Morgan agrees that there are great advantages to this kind of service." You get the picture, and so will your customers.

Strategize Your Stories

Many salespeople share how others have used their product, but they fail to think about *why* they're telling the story or *how* it will benefit the customer and the sales process. Before telling any story, ask yourself these questions:

* Why am I telling this story?
* What's the intended impact?
* Does it serve a purpose?
* Is there a *link* to my customer's emotional motivator? Does it solve a problem or overcome an objection?
* Is it structured in a way to hold the customer's attention?
* What's the punch line, and is that punch line memorable?

The best stories are authentic *and* compelling. Whether you're selling solar power, copiers, software, vacations, or consulting by the hour, follow these five rules of a good third-party story:

1. **The story must serve a purpose.**

   Quite simply, ask yourself, "Why am I telling this story? What impact do I want it to have on my audience?" A story must serve one of the following purposes:

   * Hit an emotional buying motive.
   * Solve a customer's potential problem.
   * Overcome an objection.
   * Build credibility.

   Stories help you connect emotionally with your customer and link what's important to them with your product. Remember, logic causes us to think, emotions cause us to act. Advertisers employ this concept masterfully.

2. **The story must be based on truth.**

   Only when you share examples of real people and real experiences will your stories resonate as authentic. According to expert speaking coach and Stanford lecturer, Lee Eisler, it's important when telling a story that you relive it as you tell it.[5] Put yourself in the moment that the event occurred. When I tried this, it made a big impact on the power of my stories. I realized I had been telling some of my stories for so long that they seemed to lack authenticity.

But what happens when you have the opposite problem? How do you get stories if you're new to a company or new to sales? Believe me; I know how frustrating being the new kid on the block can be.

CREATE A STORY VAULT

When I first started in sales, I didn't know what I didn't know and I didn't have a vault of stories like others did. Then one day, I overheard Mark's story. It was fantastic. It made the customers tear up every time he told it. So I asked him, "Mark, do you mind if I tell your story and simply say, 'One of our sales reps, Mark, has a customer and . . .'"?

He was delighted.

I asked every single sales rep the same exact question. I wrote down their stories in a little black book and categorized them.

Column A: Stories that hit a direct buying motive (DBM).
Column B: Stories that solved a problem.
Column C: Stories that overcame an objection.
Column D: Stories that create credibility.

I wrote them down. I refined every word. I learned that the words I chose had a great impact on how they landed with the customers emotionally. For example, when I described food, it was much more appealing to talk about the chocolate soufflé with the hot molten caramel filling than to say *good food*. This strategy had a huge payoff for me.

Thanks to modern technology, it's much easier to create a story vault. You can digitize your stories, including pictures of your customers, to create a story bank. You should have 30 to 40 great third-party stories. Categorize them, practice, and if they're not yours, tell them with as much passion as you can muster.

3. **The story must be relevant.**

   Don't tell your CEO customer from New York City that he reminds you of Bernie Hansen, a farmer from Nebraska. Stories only resonate with customers if they can hear them and think, "Me too! I'm just like so and so—obviously I would have the same good experience."

4. **The story shouldn't be about you.**

   Look, *you're* supposed to use and love your product. You're selling it. Effective stories are endorsements from other customers who've received emotional or financial value from your product.

5. **The story must be specific.**

   Have you ever noticed that the more specific a story or claim is, the more credible it sounds?

   Just as specific praise for accomplishment is more effective than a generalization, stories with specifics are more powerful. Attorneys, advertisers, and top salespeople know that specificity engenders believability. For example, which testimonial seems more credible?

   "Our power dialer is the best in the world for creating customer contacts."

   Or:

   "By using qualified leads upfront and calling more selectively, the power dialer we sell typically increases conversion rate by more than 35 percent."

   Use names, dates, and places whenever possible. There's a line about journalists worth repeating: The good ones don't just report that there was dog in the street. They get the name of the dog. The more specific, the more believable the story will be.

The more believable, the more it will emotionally resonate with your customer.

Quote percentage increases and decreases: "32.5 percent" is a much more credible number than "more than 50 percent." Get the exact numbers and use them to build credibility into your stories.

Stories aren't just a list of events and happenings, they take on the meaning that we give them, and they humanize and unite us. Stories help us understand the world around us. Events in and of themselves don't have meaning; rather, they take on the meaning we give them. Make your stories credible, authentic, compelling, and heartfelt, and you'll not only sell more, you'll have a better time doing it.

CHAPTER 9

Removing Resistance Takes Persistence

Universal Truth #9: As soon as a prospect displays resistance, most salespeople drop the price, modify the terms, or otherwise change the offer. But the truth is: It's only when someone is in a receptive emotional state that you can close. This section will include strategies about keeping customers receptive, isolating the toughest customer objections, and uncovering the real and final objection so you can close more deals more quickly.

When Did You Buy the Tacos?

As my husband will be delighted to tell you, I am a horrible cook. The good news is that there are a couple of dishes I make well. One of them is buffalo tacos. There are a couple of steps I follow. I write out the ingredients I'll need—taco shells, onions, cilantro, cheese, avocado, and, of course, buffalo meat. Then, I head to the market. I arrive at the grocery store, select the various items, place them in my cart, and proceed to check out.

Question: At what point did I buy the buffalo meat?

Some people tell me, "When you checked out at the cash register."

Others say, "When you took it off the shelf and placed it in your cart."

The right answer: before I even left my home, at the moment I *decided* to buy it.

The point is that your clients often decide to buy your product well before you ask them. At each step along the way, however, they are evaluating the buying decision they've already made. This means that selling isn't just closing the deal; it's actually not lousing up the deal the customer has already accepted (but hasn't told you about yet).

Most salespeople need to shift their perspective when it comes to closing. Too many think a magic close will win them the deal. They say things like: "Give me a good close for 'I want to think about it,'" or "Help me deal with 'We love it, but we need to run it through human resources, accounting, or the lawyer.'"

Selling isn't that simple. Once the ship is sunk, an anchor won't do you any good.

Before you even think about closing, you need to study each sales step we've discussed so far. More than that, get in the habit of constantly checking in with your own emotional state. Are you radiating empathy, curiosity, and responsibility?

To perform with confidence at the close, realize that customers are probably still deciding when they push back on price or another concern. Initial resistance is rarely real. They haven't placed the buffalo in the basket, but they may have taken it off the shelf and just need to read the label!

To effectively handle customer resistance, it's essential to know:

1. The six core objections to purchasing anything.
2. The science that explains why customers give salespeople excuses.
3. Three techniques to move past excuses and identify the real objection.
4. Critical closing strategies.

In this chapter, I'll share all four.

How Will I Come Up With Rebuttals for All Those Objections?

In our live Closers Workshop seminar, I start out with an assignment: "Write out every objection you've heard in the last six months." Participants love this! I play The Rolling Stones' "(I Can't Get No) Satisfaction" and everybody gets juiced.

After sorting themselves into groups of five, they write their objections out on a white sheet of butcher paper. Invariably, each group asks for more paper. The intensity increases. Soon each group has laid out 25 to 35 reasons their customers won't buy. Next, they tape the sheets up on the walls, a wallpaper of customer concerns.

Some participants become noticeably uneasy. "How can I possibly learn rebuttals for all of those objections?" someone asks.

"Sheeesh! No wonder I haven't been selling so much lately," says another.

In that moment, I reveal the startling truth:

"Of all the objections you've ever heard to buying anything, there are only six *real* objections. And by the end of the seminar, you'll learn how to answer all six."

There is a palpable sigh of relief.

Excuses vs. Objections: What's the Difference?

After I divulge the six real objections, salespeople want to know: "Where's 'I need to think about it?' Why isn't 'Send me a proposal' one of the six? Didn't you forget something?"

That's when I explain that these kinds of statements—"I want to think about it," "We need to check with accounting," "We're just gathering information"— are almost always an *excuse*. Customers use them to mask one of the six real objections.

To close effectively, you must start by learning the difference between an excuse and a real objection.

An excuse is a reason your customer invents so they don't have to buy. Excuses are sometimes real, but more often they're defense mechanisms. An objection, on the other hand, represents the customer's true concern. Both excuses and objections can be easily overcome, but they require different approaches. Learning strategies to distinguish between the two—and overcome them both—is key to your sales success.

Just as there's a seemingly infinite number of colors in the world—did you know we can see 10 million colors?—customer objections may seem endless.

But just as every hue is some combination of the three primary colors, there are only six real objections. I suggest you write down the most common objections you hear. Then, match them up to the six that I am about to show you. If you find that most of what you hear from customers turn out to be excuses, that's great news. Why? Because as we just saw, excuses are pretexts—you mustn't respond to them as though they're real. I'm going to teach you how to move through every possible excuse to expose your customer's core issue. Only then can you make the sale.

The Six Real Objections

1. **There's no need:** "No-need" objections result from one of two possibilities. First, your product legitimately has zero value for your prospect. For example, if you tried to sell me air-conditioned shoes (yes, there is such a product), they'd be of no value to me *at any price*. I don't run the Badwater Ultramarathon in Death Valley in July, and even if I did, my air-conditioned shoes would probably melt before mile six.

    The other "no-need" scenario happens when the customer already owns a similar product that works well or that they're not currently using. Perhaps the customer has a medical condition that prohibits use of the product, or the VP of sales has just invested in a similar product or service. If you are like most people, you'll find these objections among the most difficult to overcome because the customer simply isn't sold and doesn't have the power to overcome the no-need reasoning. But there's still hope, as we will discuss shortly.

2. **It doesn't make financial sense:** Don't confuse this objection with *It's not in our budget* or *We can't afford it.* What the customer is telling you is he can achieve his objectives for a lower price or get more value for the same amount of cash outlay. Don't treat this objection as though it is a financial objection. It's not. It's about value, not financial wherewithal. Later in this chapter, I'll show you the reframing technique you can use to isolate and overcome this objection.

3. **I don't believe it will work:** The prospect has doubts about the ease of using, installing, or owning your product. Prospects who feel your offer sounds *too good to be true* will resist you and your offer. To overcome this objection, consider the customer in front of you. If he's more analytical, back away from your grand claims. Use numbers, charts, and graphs. Show him customer testimonials and white papers, and consider bringing in a higher authority. Tell the customer what your product won't do, so he'll believe what it will do.

4. **It's too confusing:** Sometimes they just don't get it. Your prospects may not have the mental bandwidth to understand how your product will fit into their work or personal life. They're asking themselves, "What sets this program apart?" or "Why do I need it in the first place?"

    Who made it too confusing? Yep, that would be you. Most likely, you dished out too much information, too fast. Why? Because you wanted to hit it and quit it—get the sale and keep moving. Slow down; you're moving too fast. Listen more, talk less. Information overload, often caused by commission-obsessed salespeople, paralyzes your prospects. *People would rather make no decision than make the wrong decision.* To minimize this objection, you should:

* Discuss the three to five key benefits of your product that matter most to your customer (based on your discovery).
* Never answer questions the customer didn't ask.
* Avoid industry acronyms and jargon.
* Summarize benefits using infographics and analogies. Say something like, "Our bonus point program works just like your airline miles."
* Give your customer the precise amount of information she needs to make a decision, no more and no less. Decide what other information needs to be discussed after she decides to purchase.

5. **It takes too much effort:** We've already talked about the fact that your biggest competition isn't a product or a person, but the status quo. The more complex your product appears, the less likely it is that your customers will choose it. When this objection surfaces, highlight customer service and support systems. Reconfirm your experience and competence. Reiterate how after a quick ramp-up period, their lives will be made much easier. People want things to be easy.

   Customers don't always spell out objections for you like you're playing a game of Scrabble. They may not say, "This takes too much effort." Often, you need to delve deeper and read between the lines.

6. **It's too much money:** Sometimes, your customer really wants your product, but legitimately can't afford it. (This isn't the same as "It doesn't make financial sense," which occurs when you haven't yet shown the value of your offering.) Be wary of this objection; it's often used as an excuse because it seems like a painless way out. The prospect may not want to hurt your feelings. In complex sales, they just stop calling you back or they may blame procurement. Research shows customers give this objection much more often than it is warranted. It's always best to isolate this objection before giving up on a sale.

Excuses

What about the hundreds of other roadblocks you get from customers when you ask them to buy? If it's not one of the six objections, it's likely an excuse.

Excuses come in different forms, depending on the product you're selling. This may seem a bit harsh, but you should think of an excuse as a type of lie. Don't be surprised. According to Pamela Meyer, who gave the famous TED Talk "How to Spot a Liar," we all lie.[1] The average person tells 10 to 100 lies per day. It starts when we're infants. Babies fake a cry to get attention and 5-year-olds lie outright ("The dog broke the vase!"; "She hit me first!") to avoid punishment. Adults tell lies to avoid confrontation ("No, that dress doesn't make you look fat!") and to put off decisions ("I'll give you a ring back in a couple of weeks").

Perhaps the pervasiveness of technology has escalated the rate and frequency of our game of Pinocchio. We say things like, "Your e-mail must have gone to my spam folder," or, "I have a GoToMeeting . . . gotta run." The truth is we're either overloaded or bored, so we lie to buffer and preserve the relationship.

Why-Oh-Why Do Your Customers Lie?

So why won't your customers fess up? Wouldn't it be easier for them to say, "You and your product stink," "You're boring me to death," or "I wouldn't trust you to switch the radio station?" Before studying the reasons, think of yourself as a consumer. Have you ever snapped off an excuse rather than sharing your real issue? Have you ever not known why you were doing the avoidance dance and yet you did it anyway? I have.

Several years back, I made an appointment with Charlie at the Land Rover dealership. After I test-drove the car, Charlie asked me to buy it—and rightly so. But something felt strange. I couldn't put my finger on it.

I did have some concerns. One was that I'd heard Land Rovers had a poor service record. When I raised this issue, Charlie dismissed my question. Not one baby negative or "Geez, let me check that out for you." All I heard were superlatives like "This is the best . . . the greatest . . . the most."

Think about it: Would *you* have told Charlie you thought he was an inflator and a hyperbolist? (Yes, I just made that word up.) Maybe not; but would you have trusted his intentions?

I didn't. Instead, I took the cowardly path and gave Charlie a lame excuse. I told him that my brother had the same model, and I had to speak to him before buying. "The problem is," I said, "he's in Belgium." So I asked for Charlie's card and never called him back.

Typically, customers won't make a decision because they're stuck. They are experiencing one of three of what I call "negative buyer emotional states." In other words, they are stuck in one of three places:

* The state of suspicion.
* The state of fear.
* The state of embarrassment.

The capital of each of those states is "indecision."

The State of Suspicion

Look out. Your prospect has no confidence in you or your company. You failed to earn his trust. Remember to use baby negatives to let prospects know you're not hiding anything. You know the brother-in-law, CFO, or parent who tells the customer what's wrong with your offer? Beat him to it. I used to love responding to the question "Can you tell me about your maintenance fees?" with "I guarantee they'll go up," or answering "Is there good resale value?" with "No, you'll try to pawn it off on your spouse in the event of a divorce." Seriously. This made prospects laugh. Then, I'd answer the question honestly and specifically.

Too many salespeople resort to puffery instead of gauging how a prospect feels about your offer, so when they fail to buy, the salesperson is blindsided. There you have it. Sorry!

The State of Fear

People would rather make no decision than make the wrong decision. "Analysis paralysis" stops companies, governments, and consumers from moving forward—often at the expense of what is best and most profitable. Customers fear the shame of making a bad decision, so they often make none at all.

THE STATE OF EMBARRASSMENT

Products and services are more complicated today than ever. But customers who don't understand your product are usually too embarrassed to tell you. I once worked with a salesperson named Marco. His presentation was three times as long as anyone else's. He assured his customer in his statement of intent that even a 5-year-old could understand his product. Guess what? His customer, not wanting to be mistaken for an exceptionally stupid 5-year-old, kept his mouth shut. No questions, no objections—and no sale!

Don't Try to Hit a Hologram

Neural research shows that we are better able to concentrate, focus, and make decisions when we aren't experiencing negative emotions. As long as your prospects are stuck in one of the three negative emotional states, they're not thinking clearly. Not only will they not make a decision, but they're probably not going to give you their real objections. Suspicion, fear, and embarrassment all spring from the amygdala. This part of the brain is focused on fight or flight—so you should expect your customers to argue with you or make an excuse and split. This response is wired into their DNA!

The question is: What can you do about it?

Amiable, Aggressive, or Respectfully Assertive

It should be obvious by now that how you sell is even more important than what you sell. Remember Suzy and Tony and their extreme approaches to sales? Suzy was our people-pleaser and Tony the hard-charging, boiler room guy.

Amiable salespeople like Suzy never ask the tough discovery questions or challenge the customers during their presentations, so they never build true urgency. They end up making concessions at the end because the customer was never really "in" the deal.

Overly aggressive salespeople like Tony turn on the push at the end of their presentations, when they should be gaining commitment and creating tension all the way through.

Contrast those two approaches with the approach of respectfully assertive salespeople who manage the emotional state of the customer throughout the entire sales process—not just at the end. They do a terrific job of building rapport, but they also know when to roll up their sleeves and ask for the order. Moreover, they can handle customer resistance at the end because they have been doing it all along.

Be assertive, but never aggressive. The following behaviors not only lose you the deal, they lose your company long-term credibility.

Don't Try This at Work!

* **Don't challenge the excuse.** When you argue with customers, you're just moving them from one negative state to another. For example, if Charlie the Land Rover dealer had either told me to get my brother on the phone or applied pressure based on false scarcity ("The price is going up tomorrow" or "This is the last one on the lot"), I would simply have moved from the state of suspicion to a new state: anger. I might even have left him with a snarky remark. So will your customers if you try to confront them.

* **Don't drop the price.** You lower your price, thinking, "If it's just cheap enough, they'll buy it." I've got news for you: If you make *anything* cheap enough (except for those air-conditioned shoes, maybe), *someone* will buy it. But not if they are in the state of suspicion. Unless you uncover and address the real objection, they'll simply stay in buying position NINE: "*Not Interested Now—or Ever.*"

Why are we so quick to drop the price? Many salespeople underestimate what their product can do for their customer or, as my colleague, Adam Robertson, says, they don't see the value and they're selling from their own pocket. You will always be better off demonstrating value than debating price. And if you compete solely on price, someone out there will beat you on price. Find out if price really is the customer's only and final objection. When you try to overcome the excuse, as my former colleague Joe McGriff puts it, "it's like trying to hit a hologram." You keep smacking at it. You can whack it from every direction, but you'll never make contact.

* **Don't just get movin' (take the next step before you've gotten the go-ahead).** Katie sells a sophisticated technology in the supply chain space. Deals can take six months to three years to close and involve multiple decision-makers. The moment Katie hears "We don't know our budget" she gets to work writing a lengthy proposal. Guess what? Three months later she hears, "This is too expensive." Katie obviously doesn't dig deep enough; if they say it's too expensive, they had a budget!

* **Don't be a doormat.** Like Suzy, you wait around for customers to call you back, tell all your friends about your big deal that's coming in any day now, and spend the commission check you haven't yet earned. Salespeople who lack confidence say things like "Let me know when you'll be able to decide," or "I'll give you my home number, feel free to call me with any questions or concerns." This isn't customer service; it's servility. Know when to say *next*.

* **Don't be desperate.** Consider the following scenario: A salesperson has just asked the customer if she's ready to make a purchase.

> **Customer:** "I'll have to run the numbers. We'll look at the budget for the year and get back to you."
>
> **Salesperson:** "But if you don't buy now, the prices are going up. We are closing out on this model and you'll have to pay more."

Customer (*irritated*): "We'll just have to take that risk."
[Sound of door slamming.]

Can you guess which state the customer is in?

If you were the customer, how would you feel? How long would it take before you'd get up and leave? The salesperson is obviously insincere, desperate, and uncompassionate. Whatever trust the salesperson created, he just sabotaged it. The salesperson needs to apply wholehearted listening. He needs to validate the customer's feelings before responding. He might also need an extended vacation.

✱ **Don't sell a hat that doesn't fit.** Last fall, I traveled to Eastern Europe with a group of executives. While visiting Heroes' Square in Budapest, a street vendor approached me and asked if I'd buy a fur hat. The conversation went like this:

> **Street vendor:** You can buy my hat for 40 euros.
> **Shari:** Can I try it on? [She hands it to me.] It doesn't fit. It's too small. Do you have another hat?
> **Street vendor:** No. It's a nice hat. It's made from beaver. Okay, 30 euros?
> **Shari:** It still doesn't fit. I won't wear it.
> **Street vendor:** Okay . . . 20 euros, plus another of the same hat.

Maybe there was a language barrier and the saleswoman didn't understand what I said. Or maybe these were her last two hats, and she just wanted to unload them and go home. The point is: To successfully sell, you must uncover the true objection and answer it. Why would I buy a hat that doesn't fit, even if it *is* cheaper? My ears were cold. I needed a hat that would cover them. Could I have torn the two hats apart and made one hat that actually fit? That's not how I wanted to spend my vacation.

Closing isn't about finding clever rebuttals to customer concerns or using sharp-angled boxing techniques. Closing is about having the compassion, patience, and heart to uncover the customer's real concern, address it, and then close the deal.

PUT IT INTO ACTION

Identify the Real Objection

Now you know the six core objections:

1. No need.
2. Doesn't make financial sense.
3. I don't believe it will work.
4. Too much effort.
5. Too confusing.
6. Money.

Take the following customer statements and place them into one of the six categories. Remember, although some of these are valid objections, others might just be excuses to conceal the real objection. Determining the real objection is not an exact science, so try your best. Every time you come up against resistance, use the six real objections as a template to figure out whether your customer is giving you an excuse or a legitimate objection. Simple awareness of the six core objections will dramatically increase your performance. Factor that in as you go through this list:

* I'll run it by the board.
* This is the first one we've seen.
* We're in the proposal-gathering stage.
* The timing isn't right.
* The kids are going to college.
* We're looking at many different options.
* This is interesting. Send me some literature and we'll get back to you.
* It's simply not in the budget right now.
* We're satisfied with who we have now.
* I don't see how we could use it right now.

- I can see the value, but it's not for me.
- This isn't my department.
- We will need to mull over the numbers.
- It's not a priority right now.
- We're cutting back.
- It's too expensive.
- We're looking for better quality.
- I had a bad experience with your company.
- We've been doing business with our current supplier for years.
- My brother is in the business.
- You have to sharpen your pencil.
- You've given us a lot think about.

Can you think of more? Every time a customer shows resistance, see if you can connect it to one of the six real objections. Then, be prepared. Create rebuttals for each of the six ahead of time that make sense for your product, company, and industry.

Uncover the Real Objection: Three Isolating Techniques

Study the following three approaches for handling objections and practice them repeatedly. Make them your own. I've watched dozens of salespeople memorize the words and then fail to deliver them with compassion and empathy.

You may be prepared to isolate objections and answer pertinent concerns, but if you become impatient or agitated, you'll never get there. Much as being conscious of emotions helps in sales, allowing yourself to be hijacked by your own emotions is quite costly.

There is a natural human tendency—one that you have to overcome— to answer customer objections before isolating them. When closing, you must slow down. Listen. Make sure you understand the customer's point of view before you try to convince them of yours. Delivering your words with a sharp, condescending tone will never work. Your goal isn't to be right; it's to make the sale. This is not a *Gotcha!* moment.

If delivered effectively, each of these techniques will shift the customer from a negative state to a more receptive state. He will reveal his true concern and open up to your offer:

1. The "If It Were Next Week" Close

This approach stands in stark contrast to high-pressure, "This offer is only good for one day," closes. However, make no mistake, the goal is still to close the sale now or as soon as possible. Build your own variation on the following script:

Customer: We need to think about it.

Salesperson: No problem. I know this is a big decision, you may feel better taking your time. [Pause. Take out your electronic calendar or paper notebook.] How long do you feel you will need to decide?

Customer: At least a month.

Salesperson: [Pick a date about a month out. It's important to pick an exact time to follow up. It mustn't be nebulous.] How about I give you a ring then on October 24th—let's say 9 a.m.?

Customer: That could work.

Salesperson: Okay, I'll jot that down.

At this point, your customer will visibly relax. In his mind, he won't have to make a decision today, ask questions, or try to understand anything complicated. He's off the hook! More importantly, he's moved from his amygdala to his more resourceful brain (iguana to party hat). He can think more clearly. He may access concerns that he didn't even realize he had.

Here's what to do next:

Salesperson: Just out of curiosity, let's suppose it is a month from now and I call you at 9 a.m. on that morning. Are there any questions or concerns you think you might have at that time?

Customer: Well, I think we just need to do more research on your company and make certain this is the best choice for us.

Aha! You've moved from the excuse to the real objection.

This approach is powerful. It's the total opposite of what customers expect. They relax, which opens up the creative part of their brains. Now, they can pinpoint the source of their discomfort. This is a great technique to use when you hear, "I need to think about it," or, "We're not ready to decide now." It all boils down to uncovering which of the six real objections is holding your customer up so you can effectively address it. If you perform this close successfully, your customer will open up to you, and you'll be able to overcome the source of his real concerns.

Again, what's important is that you make this technique your own—as presented, this may sound a little manipulative. Your tone and delivery will be critical to your success. Don't let your hunger for a closed deal cloud your thinking or your customer's.

2. Restate Customer Concerns

Many salespeople freeze when the customer says "I need to think about it," "We need to talk to legal," or "We don't have a budget." The problem is that these excuses mask the real objection. By restating customer concerns using specific wording, you can uncover which of the six real objections the customer has.

Follow these five steps:

1. Listen intently to your customer's concern.

2. Use a "bridging statement" such as "I understand how you feel—of course this is a big decision," and then restate the concern back to your customer. Ask for validation.

3. Isolate the objection in order to make certain it's the only one.

4. Answer the objection(s).

5. Close.

Here's the five-step approach in action:

Customer: We'll need to think this over and get back to you. We're simply not prepared to make a decision.

Salesperson: I can appreciate that. This is a big decision. It sounds like you *have a few concerns* before moving forward. Is that about right?

[Don't ever repeat vague phrases like, "We need to think this over." Instead, find a way to restate "think this over" more tangibly. Why? You can deal with a *few concerns*; what you can't deal with is *I need to think about it*.]

Customer: Yeah, that's about right.

[Once you have restated the customer's concerns, you can go deeper and isolate the customer's concern using the precise restating language from earlier.]

Salesperson: Other than those *couple of concerns*, is there any other reason why you wouldn't feel comfortable moving forward on this?

Customer: No, that's it. We just need some time.

Salesperson: [Pause. This is important!]

[At this point, one of two things will happen: Either the customer will stay with a no decision or, hopefully, they will divulge the real issue.]

Customer: I'm just not certain that this will integrate with our new system. I will need to discuss it with our IT department.

Now you have an objection you can work with.

3. Deal With the Ghost in the Room

This is a terrific technique to use when your customer uses a third party as an excuse. You know what I'm talking about. It happens all the time: you're lucky enough to land a qualified prospect, you create strong rapport, your customer loves your product, and the price is right.

There's just one problem. They need to speak with their brother (or mother, or doctor, or lawyer, or board members) about it. This brother, of course, is vacationing in Italy, and can't be reached. I call this third party "the ghost in the room." (Remember: I gave this excuse to Charlie, the Land Rover dealer.)

When your customer claims they need to speak with someone else, it can be an excuse, not a real objection.

Too many salespeople challenge the customer's excuse by blurting out "Let's get the 'ghost' on the phone," or "I'm sure he'll love it—let's draw up the paperwork." What's the problem? Unless you're dealing with a product with a long sales cycle, this approach addresses the customer's excuse—not their real concern.

Next time your customer says, "I need to run this by my brother, mother, dentist, or board members," consider the following technique. The first time I saw it, I was enthralled.

Ira was selling a slot in a very upscale senior living community to an older couple in Scottsdale. The prospects, Mr. and Mrs. Bayfield, liked the idea of resort-style living: The activities, education, and entertainment went beyond anything they could have imagined.

After completing the tour, Ira asked for the order. The Bayfields assured him they were interested, but just needed to confer with their grown children.

The conversation went like this:

Mrs. Bayfield: We'll have to get back to you after we talk to our kids.

Ira: No problem. I completely understand. Just out of curiosity, if your kids don't approve this, I assume you will say no to this community?

Mr. Bayfield: Probably. We would really like to get their opinion, as they'll be the ones visiting us here.

Ira: That makes sense. Now if they say yes, will you go ahead with this?

Mrs. Bayfield: Absolutely.

Ira: Why would you want to move here? [Pause. This is the hard part, especially for salespeople. Be quiet and let them give you an answer!]

Mr. Bayfield: Well, we love the community aspect. We have friends here, and we'd rather move to a place like this now, before one of us is ill.

Do you see what happened? The Bayfields confirmed their own dominant buying motive. Ira let them realize on their own that talking to their children was unnecessary. This technique incorporates a scientific principle called cognitive dissonance: the disconnect that sets in if we feel that our actions aren't aligning with our beliefs. The Bayfields' true concern was to establish a secure environment for their old age. They saw that the act of speaking to their children first had nothing to do with their real goal. Once they recognized their cognitive dissonance, they were able to make their own decision. By asking why they'd say yes, you're forcing them to articulate all of the reasons in favor of your product. And no one wants to make a liar or of himself or herself.

PUT IT INTO ACTION

The 7 Strategies to Removing Resistance

People have resisted salespeople since the beginning of time. Just as salespeople have a default mode, prospects do, too. Their automatic response is to say, "No way, José."

Face it. People don't want to be sold. This sentiment is increasing as we live more of our lives online. According to Terry Jones, founder of Kayak.com, 98 percent of all college students would rather purchase online. They avoid salespeople at all costs. As Mike Weinberg says in *New Sales Simplified*, the fact that customers have sales resistance isn't your *fault*, but it is your *problem*.[2]

Fortunately, it is a problem that the right training can solve. Here's how:

1. Define What Concessions You're Willing to Make in Advance

What concessions are you willing to make? You had better know before heading into the close, before your adrenaline kicks in. In the heat of the moment, you might throw in your dog and the kitchen sink before you've thought through the financial ramifications of your new offer.

Clearly define discounts, upgrades, and incentives in advance of any negotiation. How far can you go? How far *should* you go? Plan what the customer will give you in return. Don't offer discounts and ask for nothing in return.

Remember, knowing what you'll concede and when you will concede are two different things. You are always better off starting with smaller concessions, and offering bigger ones as your negotiations progress. Never say, "Take it or leave it," unless you really are willing to walk away. By pre-planning, you will close more deals and appear stronger and more confident to your customer.

2. Summarize Your Offer

After I demonstrate my product to customers, I like to ask *them* to articulate how they feel about it. "What do you like about what I've shown you so far?" Ask this question aside from the obvious impediment of price: "Assuming the numbers work, what do you like about what I've shown you so far?" Make sure to ask everyone who is present. They may tell you what they like, or they may give you an objection. Either way, they'll arm you with valuable information.

3. Don't Lead With Incentives

When you lead with incentives, you lose credibility—particularly if your customer isn't already sold. You just sound desperate, which makes the customer wonder what's wrong with your product or with you. The other day, I walked into a boating store to kill time while my son was next door at a karate class. The salesmen offered to throw in water skis and a wetsuit if I purchased his boat by the weekend. The problem is that although the water skis sounded cool and the wetsuit would be good for diving, I wasn't sold on the $55,000 boat, so the bonus meant nothing to me.

4. Don't Send a Proposal or Create a Contract Until All of the Terms Are Agreed Upon by All of the Stakeholders

I bet you've heard this before: "Send me a proposal," or "Put it in writing." These statements can be an excuse. Solidify all the terms of your deal with all relevant decision-makers before committing anything to writing. If you don't, your client may change his mind or change the deal, leaving you with little wiggle room.

Also, sometimes when people ask for a proposal in writing, it's because they really want to just get you off the phone without hurting your feelings. If you sense that's what's happening, ask. If you think about selling as a quest for the truth, finding out how your prospect really feels is essential. Otherwise, you'll be writing a whole lot of proposals that no one will ever read.

5. Reframe Money Objections

I often hear customers tell salespeople that they need to check their budget, mull it over for a while, or otherwise think about the money. So here's a test. Which one of the six real objections is that?

Answer: You don't know yet.

Too many salespeople assume that these responses mean the customer can't afford your offer. But you can't *know* what his true objection is until you isolate it. Is it a question of financial sense or money?

Try this reframing technique:

Salesperson: "That makes sense. Let me ask you this: When you say you're going to mull over the numbers, will you be checking to see if our product/program saves you money or gives you more value for the money you're already spending?"

This kind of interjection lets you know the real issue, while also making the customer reconsider your product. You've highlighted the fact that your product may not in fact be less money, but it may represent a better value. It opens the door to a value discussion instead of letting that same door close on a money objection.

6. Make Certain You Have the Prospect's Full Attention

Your customer must be attentive and engaged before you ask for the sale. If you find them fussing with their cell phone or seeming otherwise distracted, stop.

A friend of mine was negotiating a strategic partnership with a successful entrepreneur.

"I made a critical mistake," he told me. "He was driving on the autobahn in Europe with his wife, and here I am on the other end of the line trying to negotiate the terms, titles, and salaries of our partnership."

The truth is, first, big deals are best made in person. I know we've got GoToMeeting, Skype, Zoom Band, and Boom, but let's get real. Nothing beats face-to-face communication. How can you pass the "smell test" if they can't smell you? Fortunately, the Internet hasn't approached the point where we can small each other online. Be grateful.

7. Save a Valuable Piece of Information For Last

Depending on your product, you may not want to show your customers everything! You've heard of saving the best for last? When you save a valuable piece of information—for example, a unique service add-on—you're holding onto a negotiation tool you may very well need.

Remember, customers are taught to say "no" before they say "yes." Unfortunately, most sales reps respond by dropping price. When you refrain from showing something valuable, you have the upper hand in the negotiation.

Ask yourself, what adds value besides price?

* Incentives.
* VIP service.
* Extended warranty.
* Bonus program.
* Increased usage.

When your customer asks for a discount, you can respond by asking which incentive he's willing to give up.

Replace the Hard Work With the Heart Work

Buyers won't tolerate high pressure or false urgency. Know why your prospect is objecting. I don't mean the made-up reason they give you, or the made-up reasons you tell yourself. I mean the honest-to-goodness *real* reason they put up initial resistance. Armed with this information, you can address their true concern and close the deal.

Keep your presentation simple and engaging so he will put the buffalo meat in his own cart. If he gives you an excuse, find out the real problem. What state is he in? Gently lead him out of the state of indecision and into the state of contentment. Today's customers don't want to be closed, they want to be led. When you ask for the order, you're not presenting them with hard work. You're giving them just the right amount of patience, compassion, and *heart work*.

Now that you know how to change the emotional state of the buyer, our last universal truth shifts our gaze inward once again. When we're in conversations with customers, are we looking for what's right or what's wrong? It's a vital distinction for salespeople, and you'll learn all about it in the next chapter.

CHAPTER 10

Looking for Wrongs Never Makes You Right

Universal Truth #10: Every day, in every encounter, you have a choice. You can look for what's right about that person or experience—what's valuable or productive—or you can look for what's wrong. When you're interacting with your associates or your customers, don't look for reasons why they won't buy. Look instead for reasons why they will buy. Whatever you look for, be certain you'll find it!

If Only I Had a Trampoline

When I was a little girl in Northern California, I wanted a trampoline more than anything in the world. I whined to my parents, "If only I had a trampoline, I'd never be bored." But when I got a trampoline, nothing really changed. Well, not *nothing*: The mantra changed, slightly. It became, "If only I had a moped, I'd never be bored."

When I was 16, my family moved to a sunny beach town, and things changed again. In Southern California, if you were pretty, you had it all. Life was perfect. "Pretty" meant long straight hair, perfect white teeth,

Kahlua-colored long legs, and big open eyes. I was short with wavy hair and little eyes.

I had a group of best friends. We called ourselves the YMCA: "You, me, Colleen, and Adams." Lisa Adams was so beautiful we called her "Beautiful Lisa." Beautiful Lisa was homecoming queen and class president. Beautiful Lisa looked like Brooke Shields and her boyfriend was captain of the football team. What would it be like to be Beautiful Lisa?

My mantra changed again. If only I looked like Beautiful Lisa, I'd finally be content.

It was a blustery December evening in 1979. The YMCA was having our ritual Christmas gathering in Lisa's tree house in the Palos Verdes Hills. We were on our second bottle of white wine.

"What's it like to be so beautiful?" Kathy asked Beautiful Lisa. She was the "Me" in the YMCA.

We all leaned forward to hear the answer. Each of us had always wanted to ask the question, but none of us had had the courage.

Lisa was silent for several breaths.

"It's just a thing," she said.

Huh?

"Like Colleen is a beautiful dancer," she explained, "and Kate has this magnetic personality, Karen is tenacious, and Shari is so creative. We each have a special something. Each of you is amazing."

That was when I realized just how amazing Lisa really was. Lisa and I had always had a sort of competitive thing, or at least I had had it with her. And here she was, at 17, so elegant and full of grace, reflecting back all the light we'd shone on her.

"That thing, in and of itself, doesn't make you happy." Lisa went on. "I still have problems. Lots of them."

It wasn't until I was an adult that I realized that, like all of us, Lisa had her own hurdles to overcome. But long before I understood the full depth of Lisa's lesson, she helped me see there was no use in pining my life away, dreaming of all my "if onlys." I learned to stop obsessing about what was missing, and to start thinking about what was right.

It changed everything.

When you believe that you have enough money, love, resources, and support to realize your dreams, you will attract even greater abundance. The people who turn their lives around are the ones who change, first and foremost, their attitude. If you're happy within, you can be happy without.

Reverse the Formula of "Happily Ever After"

We're taught as children that if we marry the prince or princess, secure the killer job, and have 2.5 kids, we'll live happily ever after. Myth buster: There is no "happily ever after." However, there *are* ways to train your brain to become more positive.

Rather than banking on the hope that one day you'll be successful, at which point all your problems will go away, you need to reverse the formula. Optimism fuels productivity. Think about that for a moment: You can actually rewire your brain to function more positively and optimistically. The rituals to achieve optimism are the subject of this chapter. Specifically, you will learn how to:

* Leverage the neuroscience of positivity to achieve your goals.
* Overcome the fear factor.
* Practice six rituals that promote optimism.

In short, optimism takes effort. Remember, the fulfillment that accompanies excellence—from achieving mastery and hitting your goals—is more powerful than the fleeting happiness you feel after eating an ice cream cone or sipping a margarita on the shore. True fulfillment isn't about being there; it's about *getting* there. Or as master motivator Earl Nightingale quoted Cervantes' *Don Quixote*, "The road is better than the inn."

The Neuroscience of Positivity

When you're feeling happy, well-rested, and positive, you're more productive and full of ideas. You make more deals because your positivity is contagious.

On the other hand, when you're fearful or angry, you feel stuck and unable to problem-solve. You view your customers as unqualified or too difficult to deal with. Why are they wasting your precious time (when you could do just as good a job wasting it without their help)?

To paraphrase American happiness researcher author and speaker, Sean Anchor, when you feel positive, dopamine floods your system and not only makes you happier, but turns on the learning centers in your brain, making you more receptive to new ideas and solutions. Our brains are then able to work harder, faster, and more intelligently.

Overcoming the Fear Factor

So, that all *sounds* good. But how do you stay positive when the mortgage isn't paid, and you haven't made a sale in weeks? How do you break through the natural fear, anxiety, and resistance to achievement?

One of my favorite books is *The War of Art* by Steven Pressfield. The major theme is that when attempting any worthwhile endeavor—anything you'd love to accomplish—you will encounter resistance. It's often easier not to try than to risk failure. What separates professionals from everyone else is that even though they are fearful of something, they never resist trying everything. They do whatever it takes.

"Resistance is directly proportional to love," writes Pressfield. "If you're feeling massive Resistance, the good news is that it means there's tremendous love there, too. The more Resistance you experience, the more important your unmanifested art/project/enterprise is to you."[1]

Pressfield goes on to say the professional has learned that success—like happiness—comes as a by-product of work. The professional concentrates on the work, and allows rewards to come or not come.

The more passionate you are about your goals, the more internal resistance you will face. The more passionate you are, the more you must pursue optimism.

I am not suggesting an inauthentic "fake it till you make it" strategy. Happiness isn't a smile you plaster on your face; it's not fishing stories that you tell while backslapping a wincing stranger. Happiness doesn't arrive suddenly in your life. It's a byproduct of many different specific actions and rituals that override your mind's natural propensity to fear (more about those rituals in a moment).

Intriguingly, the quest for happiness competes with our hardwiring for survival. Remember how we talked about the amygdala in Chapter 9? Our fight-or-flight mechanism is a repository for past trauma, fear of failure, and archaic and perceived threats. Fight-or-flight mode is useful if you're fighting off a mountain lion, but it's destructive when your own internal soundtrack gets stuck on a loop of perceived threats. It is nearly impossible to cultivate optimism when we are stuck in survival mode. Our logical mind disengages and our heart closes.

Minor stress is proven to be helpful to achievement, but finding the right balance between good stress and harmful stress is a challenge you'll face for the rest of your life. Looking for what's right means consciously choosing rituals and actions that lead you away from fear and toward optimism. It means leaving blame and rationalization at the door and making a life worth living. It means leaving the ranks of uncounted amateurs and, in Pressfield's phrase, "going pro."

Six Rituals for a Happy Life

Sometimes we think there's a magic bullet that will catapult us to happiness and success. We're frantically looking for a magic powder, a new pill, or the latest diet of clever closes. I hate to disillusion you, but the truth is there is no *one thing* that will bring you happiness.

Mastering happiness is the same as mastering any skill. Whether you're a professional artist, musician, or athlete, it takes persistence and time to become a master. You need to do a lot of little things right; it requires tireless determination and consistency in your attitude and efforts.

This principle became even more evident to me on a trip to the North Shore of Maui. I was captivated with a Koa wood bowl. I wanted to own it. The price tag had the number *five* on it. I realized that $5.00 couldn't be the price in this fine store. Could it be $500.00? Feeling a bit embarrassed, I waited for the salesperson to greet me. "How much for the bowl?" I asked.

Without a pause he replied, "It's $5,000."

I was floored.

"$5,000?" I asked, suddenly happy to simply admire it instead of feeling compelled to own it. "I'm curious: How long did it take the artist to create this $5,000 bowl?"

Without flinching, the man replied, "It took him 36 years."

When he saw my look of confusion, he explained, "Thirty-six years to be *good enough* to create it in four hours. This artist is a master craftsman."

I didn't buy it, but the lesson I got for free was priceless. At that moment, I knew that the salesperson was telling me the same thing I had been telling sales teams for years: When you're a master, you don't think of the sales process as merely the time you're with the customer. You practice rituals and create positive habits in every aspect of your life.

I define *rituals* as automatic actions and behaviors that you perform consistently. You no doubt have rituals that you perform every day, whether you're aware of them or not. You might check your e-mail when you wake up. Maybe you line up your top prospects to contact first. Or you crank up your favorite motivational song on your way to work.

Your sales process begins long before you meet the customer. Amateurs turn it on the moment they greet their customers. Professionals know that everything they do every day will impact their performance. Olympic athletes don't decide to turn it on once they're competing for the gold. They practice for hours daily, get proper nutrition and rest, and visualize their success for years before they actually compete.

It can be a real challenge to wake up happy everyday; that's why you need to make a conscious choice to incorporate rituals of happiness into your daily practice. Positivity is a skill. Like a golf game, it must be examined, practiced, and perfected. Make these small rituals a part of your life and I guarantee you'll see a big impact:

* Believe it before you see it.
* Practice gratitude.

* Create deeper connections, not just more of them.
* Practice "constructive delusion."
* Stop solving problems.
* Find your purpose.

1. Believe It Before You See It

Unknowingly, I put the "happiness first" theory to the test several years ago when my co-manager, Dave, and I headed up a brand new sales operation in Park City, Utah. In late December, 1993, we'd just recruited a sales team of the best and brightest, and we were debating a theme for our upcoming holiday party. The tradition in our organization was to award top performers with trophies, accolades, and champagne to celebrate the past years successes, but of course, this type of commemoration wasn't possible for us this year. As a new group, what successes did we have to celebrate?

I'm not certain who had the idea first, but it was a darn good one: What if we pretended it was a year in the future? We'd celebrate the sales team's *future* accomplishments *today*.

Of course, congratulations were in order for everyone. We bought banners, hats, cupcakes, balloons, and party favors. Big signs at the entry read "Happy New Year 1995." But the best part was the trophies. We made trophies for each salesperson and inscribed them with the words, "Congratulations! Top Performer of the Year, 1995."

As salespeople and their families entered the ballroom, we poured champagne into fancy flutes. We presented the entire team with an award for best resort of the year, and congratulated ourselves for pulling together as a team and crushing an all-time sales record.

"Congratulations, Linda. Great year! You did it!"

"Larry, nice work. You're amazing. Is this your wife? Thank you, Hanna, for all your support over the past year!"

At first, people were confused. "You've got the wrong year," they said. "I haven't even sold anything yet."

It wasn't long before the game became clear, and everyone joined in.

Thunderous applause accompanied each trophy presentation. One woman, Sally, became teary-eyed as she accepted her award. "I want to thank the leadership team, the administrative department, and the rest of the academy." Sniff-sniff.

That night was an epic success, but even better were the actual sales results at the end of the year. Our site was number one in the entire company and we were written up in an industry magazine as being the top ownership resort in the world! Was it coincidence? I think not. Sally and the rest of the team not only felt successful from day one, they focused on a goal bigger than themselves. They allowed the feeling of success to energize them and they all took pride in their contribution to meeting their team goals, not simply in their own prize at the end.

2. Practice Gratitude

Gratitude is the parent of all other optimism tools. Research shows it's physically impossible to appreciate someone and be in fear at the same time. Think of gratitude as the antidote to fear and feelings of lack.

Engaging in a simple gratitude exercise is one of the most effective methods of improving your overall well-being, says Dr. Dan Baker, author of *What Happy People Know* and a proponent of the positive psychology movement.[2] Dr. Baker developed the Appreciation Audit, a famous exercise designed to enhance gratitude. It's pretty simple. You just write down three things you feel grateful for each day. For example, today, I might write *my dog Mamie*, *my family*, and *pedicures*. The next day I may write *living in Park City, french fries,* and *my mother.* Other positive psychology experiments, like engaging in small acts of kindness throughout the day, have also been shown to boost happiness.

This happiness tonic shouldn't surprise you, once you're aware of it.

Next time you're at an event full of sales people, watch how the feeling in the room shifts when the leader thanks individuals around the room.

One of my son's friends lost his mother to cancer a few years back. He was only 6 years old, when it happened. Imagine, if you can bear to, the despair that level of grief can heap on a child. His pain and fear were monstrous.

His family clustered around him, and someone told him to think about three things he was grateful for each day. Each night, before going to bed and after saying his prayers, he mustered up the energy to do it. At first, it was difficult. What could he possibly be grateful for? His mother was stolen from him and there was nothing he could have done to save her. He gave up the first night and shook in his sleep.

Two nights later, he found himself able to say he was grateful for his finger paints, and also maybe hamburgers. A week later, he could say, "My dog Roscoe and the big oak tree out back." Weeks later, and he could say, "My daddy, and my stepmother, and my friends, and my future."

By taking note of what we're grateful for, we remove ourselves from the fear center in our brains, allowing us to rewire our neuro-pathways toward a better life.

Practicing gratitude means:

* **Conducting an appreciation audit.** Make a list of what you appreciate about your product, your customers, and coworkers. Stop focusing on what stinks about your job. Think about or write about this daily for 30 days and see what happens to your optimism level. Research shows that

when you maintain a gratitude journal, you increase your happiness.

* **Saying "thank you."** Think for a moment about the genuine joy you receive when you pause and say "thank you." Count the things, people, and circumstances for which you are grateful. In 2014—the year of Facebook's 10th anniversary—CEO and founder Mark Zuckerberg revealed that he was challenging himself to write one "well-considered thank-you note every day, via e-mail or handwritten letter."

"It's important for me, because I'm a really critical person," Zuckerberg told *Bloomberg Businessweek*. "I always kind of see how I want things to be better, and I'm generally not happy with how things are, or the level of service that we're providing for people, or the quality of the teams that we built."[3]

"Thank you" forces your brain to focus on what's right. You may say "thank you" before you greet your guest, go out on a walk in nature, or during prayer and meditation. Saying "thank you" will elevate your mood and create the mental mindset you'll need to tackle your day.

3.   *Create Deeper Connections, Not Just More of Them*

I wish I had a dollar for every person who has more than 5,000 Facebook friends, but is still alone on a Friday night. If I did, I'd take them all out to a big Friday night dinner! (Okay, maybe at Taco Bell. This could get expensive.) To paraphrase speaker and author Shasta Nelson, although social media connection is at an all-time high, deep human connection between individuals is at an all-time low. Social media companies have responded by creating groups and algorithms to help us connect with more people *just like us*—with the same hobbies, interests, and political affiliations. We fill our networks with so-called friends, but many of us remain unfulfilled.

The power of human connection is well-documented and critical to our health and happiness, and the need for it begins at an early age. Research shows that children raised in orphanages without skin-to-skin interaction are at extreme risk for behavioral, emotional, and social problems. Deprivation of touch leads to children with smaller brains, lower body weights, and increased stress levels.[4]

Take time to grow and nurture positive friendships in and out of work. These relationships don't move you away from your life's work—they help you build a more meaningful life.

I once worked with a saleswoman named Nan Curtain. She not only forged deep relationships with her customers, she created a community among them. She introduced new customers to repeat customers, set up golf games, and fostered new business partnerships. Nan's ability to create deep connections with and between her customers earned her the top sales spot every year.

For your own sake, nurture the deep relationships you already have and, if appropriate, help your customers forge bonds, too. Encouraging genuine community makes you more than a salesperson—it makes you *a person* who happens to sell.

4. Practice "Constructive Delusion"

At the Town and Country Jeep dealership in Long Island, as at every dealership on the planet, all of the salespeople gather around the whiteboard to look at their numbers for the month. A good month is 15 cars sold. That's when the dealership and Chrysler bonuses kick in.

Jason Mascia is less than half the age of most of the sales-people there, but has doubled everyone else's sales volume. Whereas most of the sales guys strive for 15 cars per month, Jason shoots for 30 or 40.

When the other salespeople were asked what Jason did differently, they spoke in platitudes like, "He's a good-looking kid," or, "He makes a friend." But according to Sean Cole of *This American Life*, who followed Jason around for a week, there's much more to it than that.

Sean called Jason's success "Constructive Delusion."[5] You've heard the expression, "Do you see the glass as half-empty or half-full?" Jason knows a certain percentage of customers will walk out without buying anything, but it doesn't faze him. He not only doesn't see the glass as half-full, he sees it as overflowing. He views each and every customer as a potential buyer, no matter who they are or where they're from. Call him delusional, but it seems to serve him well.

After talking to thousands of salespeople about their success, I've found this phenomenon is common among the very best. They not only look for reasons their customers will purchase; they're dumbfounded when they don't. In short, you will see what you expect to see.

There's a scientific phenomenon that explains this idea called "confirmation bias." Cognitive researchers have found that we have an unconscious tendency to seek out and readily accept information that confirms our preconceptions, and to ignore, distort, or discount information that contradicts (or disconfirms) them.[6]

In other words, when you begin a sales call believing that engineers don't buy or that human resources people always muck up the deal, you wind up looking for signs that confirm your beliefs. The problem is that when you do this, you act on those negative signs and often lose the deal.

5. Stop Solving Problems

We live in a problems-solving culture. We look for what's wrong with people and ideas, rather than what's right. Many psychologists focus on our mental disorders and not on the areas of life where we're doing well. The news spends most of their time on disasters, murders, and political disarray, and medical doctors consistently look for disease rather than health and wellness.

Salespeople do this when they fall into a slump. We try to gauge: What am I doing wrong? Why did I miss that deal? Although these are useful questions and questions that *should* be asked—long after the deal is finished—don't forget to ask yourself what you did *right*. Remember the last time you were on fire. What did you do right? Can you quantify it? Can you visualize it? If all you do is dissect problems, you'll move further away from solutions.

Recently, I agreed to do pro bono work for a start-up that needed to call 148 hospitals to complete an important survey. They hired a salesperson, Veronica, to make the calls. After six weeks, she felt frustrated and defeated.

"No one will return my calls," she said. "I have left three and four voicemails and they refuse to call me back. Some of them have mailboxes that are full, so I can't even leave a message!"

I asked Veronica what her penetration goal was. She replied her boss's goal was 50 percent, but hers was 70 percent.

"Where are you now?" I asked.

"Only 18 percent," Veronica said. She felt like a failure.

Instead of focusing on those who didn't participate, I asked her what she did to facilitate the 18 percent. Her whole demeanor changed as she shared what she did and what obstacles she overcame. Victoria explained that when she did well, she thanked the customers for taking the time, she listened to them discuss their challenges even outside the workplace, and she planned to tackle her most difficult clients first thing in the morning before getting sidetracked with e-mail and other projects.

What was the result? She went on to secure another 40 percent in two weeks. By focusing on what she did right, she shifted her attitude and reached her goals.

6. Find Your Purpose

Don't just ask yourself why you do what you do. Ask yourself: Who do you want to be? What gives your life meaning? This is the most important question we can ask ourselves. It's a much more important question than, "What are my goals? What actions must I take to reach them?" Everything, from your goals to your strategies, flows from knowing who you are and why you're doing something.

You may have heard of the book *Man's Search for Meaning*. If not, get it. The author, psychiatrist Viktor Frankl, was captured by the Nazis in 1942 and labored in death camps until the war ended in 1945. His family was killed in the camps. Frankl's theory, known as "logotherapy," from the Greek word "logos" (meaning), holds that our primary drive in life isn't pleasure—but the discovery and pursuit of what we personally find meaningful.[7]

What drives you deep inside? Why do you do what you do? Are you motivated by love or by fear? One of the most significant cornerstones of happiness is to know what you're best at and use those strengths to add value to something greater than yourself.

Salespeople spend the better part of their lives finding out the motivations of their customers, yet they may never stop and define their own.

My mother once visited a Baha'i Temple in Israel. After taking a tour of the temple compound, she was met at the gate by a man who asked whether she had any questions. My mother got right to the point: "What is the Baha'i belief on the purpose of life?"

"It's up to each of us to find our purpose, and that is the meaning of our life," he said. "We believe that God created the world like a large computer. God is the master of that computer and each one of us is one of the million parts of that computer. We all have a special role to play. Our job is to discover it."

Define your role. What is your purpose in this interconnected world? Once you discover your role in this world, and how it helps others, the world will conspire to help you.

I just saw an interview with Kevin Plank, the CEO of Under Armour, one of the fastest-growing American clothing companies. His purpose isn't just to make a buck or even to manufacture clothing. He's driven to put thousands of Americans back to work, to clean up violence in cities with high unemployment, and to make Baltimore a desirable city again for families and Millennials alike.[8] His purpose is not only emotional—it's bigger than him and it engages others.

Look for your core motivation: your real purpose. Are you working for your children, or perhaps to support your spouse? When your purpose aligns with your talent, you have the best chance for success. Find meaning that's bigger than you. Here are some ideas to trigger your thoughts:

* **If you earned an extra $5,000 per month, what you would do with it?** More travel? Save for retirement? Buy cool stuff? Donate more to charity? Once you have an answer, keep asking, "And then what? Let's say I could do all that stuff. Then what would I do?" If you keep asking, you uncover your Third-Level motivators: to spend more time with family, to increase security, to pay for the kids' education. When you uncover your core motivators, you start to uncover why you do what you do. Your *why* will move you past fear and rejection.

* **What do you want your obituary to say?** In his book *The Road to Character,* David Brooks discusses the difference between "resume virtues" and "eulogy virtues." Resume virtues, Brooks reminds us, are those skills you bring to the marketplace—qualities like drive, competition, and gregariousness.

  The eulogy virtues, on the other hand, are the ones people will talk about at your funeral. Were you kind, honest, empathetic, and loyal? "Many of us are clearer on how to build an external career than on how to build inner character," writes Brooks.[9]

  What do you want your legacy to be? How do you want to be remembered? Do your actions line up with your values? These are the virtues you need today to stand out above your competitors. The combination of character and skills are what you need to radiate inner confidence and outward success.

* **What makes you forget to eat and sleep?** We've all had the experience where we're so focused on something that six hours go by and we say, "Oh my God, I forgot to eat my tuna fish." Every job has its downside. I dislike paperwork. You may love selling, but hate entering data. But as you master the less glamorous tasks, you will find more joy in all of your work. When joy is a byproduct of your labors, rather than your aim, you will reap greater rewards.

Top performers understand the difference between happiness and fulfillment. It took me a while to learn they aren't the same. Happiness is fleeting. It has to do with external events, shiny things, and symbols. And, to the extent that we reach for happiness through material possessions, we'll fall short of ever achieving either.

Many people engage in their craft solely to make money, *to win the deal,* or to buy the next new thing. "If only I had a

Mercedes Benz, I'd never be bored." "If I could just close that big deal, my life would be perfect." "If only I could change companies, I would be successful." And on and on. Their "if onlys" direct their every move and control their every thought.

Find your true purpose and you'll grow the optimism you need for true fulfillment and success.

A Rare Talent

I have a confession to make. I started out as a less-than-mediocre salesperson. I spent five years selling very little and making even less. And then I had one extraordinary week. It was a little while after my boss and mentor, Greg, asked me what I was willing to give up to reach my goals.

I was working late when Greg approached me and said, "Shari, I need to see you before you leave tonight."

I finished writing up the client contract I was working on and started the long walk down to his basement office. My mouth was dry. I found myself subconsciously trying to control my strangely ragged breaths. I couldn't imagine what I'd done; I'd never been called into the boss's office before. I had to keep my lips from quivering; I couldn't make eye contact.

I needn't have worried. He sat me down, closed the office door, looked me in the eye, and said, "Shari, I've been in this business for 18 years. I've been watching you. You have a *rare talent*. If you keep learning and training, you have the ability to be number one in the industry!"

I couldn't believe it. Not only was I *not* in trouble, I was getting praise I'd never gotten before! "If you keep up the good work, and invest in a little bit of training, you have the ability to be one of the best salespeople this industry has ever seen," he said.

I left Greg's office with my head held high, reenergized, and excited. The next morning, I arrived extra early—clearly, I had all this talent I needed to nurture. I bought every book on sales strategy, psychology, and decision-making I could find.

At the end of the year, I was the number-one salesperson at our resort. The second year, I was the number-one salesperson in all of Marriott.

I'd worked harder than I ever had in my life, and all the way, with each accomplishment, Greg congratulated me on my "rare talent." Eventually, he made me a manager.

Two months later, I found my "rare talent" didn't extend to managing; I was a miserable failure at my new post. Half my team liked me, the other half hated me, and those sides would flip flop back and forth every day. I couldn't do anything right. I finally walked into Greg's office and threw up my hands. "I'm not cut out for management stuff," I said.

"What took you so long?" was Greg's reply.

"When you were a salesperson," he continued, "you came in asking for training and help almost daily. Now that you're a manager, you seem to think you should already know it all."

My eyes welled up.

"Are you going to quit?" he asked, and watched me shake my head through my tears. "Or do you want me to help you? Do you want me to teach you how to be the world's greatest sales manager?"

I nodded.

"Okay, listen," he said, "You're going to have many salespeople work for you throughout your career. Some will be good. Some won't. But when you find one that's willing to learn, even if they're not that good, sit them down, close your office door, look them in the eye, and tell them that they have a *rare talent*. Tell them that with a little bit of training, they have the ability to become number one in the industry."

I was furious.

"Are you telling me all this time you've been telling me I had a rare talent, and you didn't mean it?"

Greg laughed so hard he just about fell off his chair. "What difference did it make?"

Suddenly, I got it. It didn't matter if I'd had a "rare talent" in the beginning or not. It didn't matter if Greg was just making it up. What mattered was that Greg had the rare ability to make me believe in myself.

Look for the good in yourself. You have to believe in you, before you can expect your clients to believe in you.

Every day, in every encounter, you have a choice. You can look for what's right or you can look for what's wrong. To get trust, give trust. To earn respect, give respect. To be applauded for your talent, look for talent in others. The happiness that comes from excellence cannot be bought; the joy derived from sharing your heart cannot be measured.

Building skill matters, but building character matters more.

NOTES

Introduction

1. Ferris Jabr, "Why Your Brain Needs More Downtime," *Scientific American*, October 15, 2013, www.scientificamerican.com/article/mental-downtime/.
2. "Habits: How They Form And How To Break Them," *NPR*, March 5, 2012, www.npr.org/2012/03/05/147192599/habits-how-they-form-and-how-to -break-them.
3. David Mayer and Herbert M. Greenberg, "What Makes a Good Salesman," *Harvard Business Review,* July 2006, https://hbr.org/2006/07/what-makes-a -good-salesman.
4. Kai Ryssdal "Goldfish have longer attention spans than Americans, and the publishing industry knows it," *Marketplace*, February 11, 2014, www.marketplace .org/2014/02/11/business/goldfish-have-longer-attention-spans-americans-and -publishing-industry-knows-it.
5. Linda Sivertsen and Danielle LaPorte, "Robert McKee: Story is Everything," podcast audio, *Beautiful Writers Podcast,* MP3, 1:00:00, March 19, 2016, https:// itunes.apple.com/us/podcast/beautiful-writers-podcast/id1047012231?mt=2.
6. Zig Ziglar, *See You At The Top* (New York: Simon & Schuster, 2009).
7. Dan Levitin, "Why the modern world is bad for your brain," *The Guardian*, January 18, 2015, www.theguardian.com/science/2015/jan/18/modern-world-bad -for-brain-daniel-j-levitin-organized-mind-information-overload.

Chapter 1: Growth Trumps Technique

1. Renee Sylvestre-Williams, "Why Your Employees Are Leaving," *Forbes,* January 30, 2012, www.forbes.com/sites/reneesylvestrewilliams/2012/01/30/why-your -employees-are-leaving/#32f4e1683a04.

2. Carol Dweck, *Mindset: The New Psychology of Success* (New York: Random House, 2007), 6–7.
3. Ibid.
4. "Benjamin Franklin Biography," *Biography*, last modified November 17, 2015, www.biography.com/people/benjamin-franklin-9301234.
5. Eric Greitens, *Resilience: Hard-Won Wisdom for Living a Better Life* (New York: Mariner Books, 2015), 110.
6. Mark Goulston, *Just Listen: Discover the Secret to Getting Through to Absolutely Anyone* (New York: AMACOM, 2015), 55–57.
7. Jonah Lehrer, "The Itch of Curiosity," *Wired*, August 3, 2010, www.wired.com /2010/08/the-itch-of-curiosity/.
8. Interview with author. Quote used with permission.
9. Kees de Jong, "Maria Joao Pires—expecting another Mozart concerto during a lunch concert in Amsterdam," YouTube video, 5:15, posted June 11, 2009, www .youtube.com/watch?v=CJXnYMl_SuA.
10. Harper Lee, *To Kill a Mockingbird* (Lippincott, PA: Harper Lee, 1960).
11. Jack Zenger and Joseph Folkman, "The Ideal Praise-to-Criticism Ratio," *Harvard Business Review*, March 15, 2013, https://hbr.org/2013/03/the-ideal-praise-to -criticism.

Chapter 2: Emotions Drive Decision-Making

1. Jason Pontin, "The Importance of Feelings," *MIT Technology Review*, June 17, 2014, www.technologyreview.com/s/528151/the-importance-of-feelings/.
2. David Mayer and Herbert M. Greenberg, "What Makes a Good Salesman," *Harvard Business Review*, July 2006, https://hbr.org/2006/07/what-makes -a-good-salesman.
3. Jason Ankeny, "How These 10 Marketing Campaigns Became Viral Hits," *Entrepreneur*, April 23, 2014, www.entrepreneur.com/article/233207.
4. Tony Robbins, "Why We Do What We Do," TED video, 21:45, filmed February 2006, posted June 2006, www.ted.com/talks/tony_robbins_asks_why_we_do _what_we_do?language=en.
5. *Mr. Holland's Opus*, film directed by Stephen Herek, (1995; Burbank, CA: Hollywood), Pictures Home Video, 1996, DVD.
6. Interview with author. Quote used with permission.

Chapter 3: Structure Facilitates Freedom

1. Eric Greitens, *Resilience: Hard-Won Wisdom for Living a Better Life* (New York: Mariner Books, 2015), 153.
2. Atul Gawande, *The Checklist Manifesto: How to Get Things Right* (New York: Metropolitan Books, 2009), 32–34.
3. Interview with author. Quote used with permission.

4. Interview with author. Quote used with permission.
5. John D. Newman and James C. Harris, "The Scientific Contributions of Paul D. MacLean (1913-2007)," *The Journal of Nervous and Mental Disease* 197 (2009): 3–5, doi: 10.1097/NMD.0b013e31818ec5d9.
6. Interview with author. Quote used with permission.
7. Mark Goulston, *Just Listen: Discover the Secret to Getting Through to Absolutely Anyone* (New York: AMACOM, 2015), 53–54.
8. Matthew Dixon and Brent Adamson, *The Challenger Sale: Taking Control of the Customer Conversation* (New York: Portfolio, 2011).

Chapter 4: In Sales, No Never Means No

1. "J.K. Rowling Biography," *Biography*, August 2, 2016, www.biography.com /people/jk-rowling-40998.
2. Dave Lifton, "The Story of the Beatles' Failed Audition for Decca Records," *Ultimate Classic Rock*, January 1, 2016, http://ultimateclassicrock.com/the-beatles -decca-records-audition/.
3. Shari Levitin, "Why You Need Emotional Intelligence to Thrive in Sales," podcast audio, *Heart and Sell*, MP3, 39:39, www.sharilevitin.com/blog-news/heart-and -sell-podcasts/colleen-stanley/.
4. Interview with author. Quote used with permission.
5. *The Wizard of Oz*, film directed by Victor Fleming, George Cukor, and Mervyn LeRoy (1939; place of publication not identified: Turner Entertainment Co., 1998), DVD.
6. Sue Rochman, "A King's Legacy," *Cancer Today*, December 5, 2011, www.cancer todaymag.org/Winter2011/Pages/yul-brynner-lung-cancer.aspx.
7. Dennis Gaffney, "Essay: What Made DiMaggio a Great Player?" *PBS*, www.pbs .org/wgbh/amex/dimaggio/sfeature/essay.html.
8. Astro Teller, "The unexpected benefit of celebrating failure," TED video, 15:32, filmed February 2016, posted April 2016, www.ted.com/talks/astro_teller_the _unexpected_benefit_of_celebrating_failure?language=en.

Chapter 5: Trust Begins with Empathy

1. Sally Kohn, "Let's try emotional correctness," TED video, 5:59, filmed October 2013, posted December 2013, www.ted.com/talks/sally_kohn_let_s_try _emotional_correctness?language=en.
2. Eric Garland, "The 'In Rainbows' Experiment: Did It Work?" *NPR*, November 16, 2009, www.npr.org/sections/monitormix/2009/11/the_in_rainbows _experiment_did.html.
3. Zig Ziglar, *See You At The Top* (New York: Simon & Schuster, 2009).
4. *Shrek*, film directed by Vicky Jenson and Andrew Adamson (2001; Glendale, CA: DreamWorks Animation, 2001), DVD.

5. Adrian F. Ward, "The Neuroscience of Everybody's Favorite Topic," *Scientific American,* July 16, 2013, www.scientificamerican.com/article/the-neuroscience -of-everybody-favorite-topic-themselves/.

6. Interview with author. Used with permission.

7. Kenneth C. Petress, "Listening: A Vital Skill," *Journal of Instructional Psychology* 26 (1999): 261, www.questia.com/library/journal/1G1-62980773/listening -a-vital-skill.

8. Paul J. Donoghue and Mary E. Siegel, *Are You Really Listening?: Keys to Successful Communication* (Notre Dame, IN: Sorin Books, 2005), 54.

9. Linda Sivertsen and Danielle LaPorte, "Robert McKee: Story is Everything," podcast audio, *Beautiful Writers Podcast,* MP3, 1:00:00, March 19, 2016, https:// itunes.apple.com/us/podcast/beautiful-writers-podcast/id1047012231?mt=2.

Chapter 6: Integrity Matters

1. Interview with author. Used with permission.

2. *Willy Wonka and the Chocolate Factory,* film directed by Mel Stuart, (1971; Burbank, CA: Warner Brothers, 2001), DVD.

3. "Connecting people and Possibilities: The History of FedEx," *FedEx,* accessed August 31, 2016, http://about.van.fedex.com/our-story/history-timeline/history/.

4. Interview with author. Used with permission.

5. Napoleon Hill, *Think and Grow Rich* (New Delhi, India: General Press, 2016), 21.

6. Liz DiAlto and Martha Beck, "EP119: Martha Beck On Life Coaching, Dreams, And Integrity," podcast audio, *Untame the Wild Soul: Spirituality | Womanhood | Sex | Relationships | Success,* MP3, 53:07, July 11, 2016, http://untameyourself .com/episode-119.

7. BrainyQuote.com, www.brainyquote.com/quotes/quotes/p/paulsamuel101705 .html.

Chapter 7: Anything That Can Be Told Can Be Asked

1. Daniel Jones, "The 36 Questions That Lead to Love," *New York Times,* January 9, 2015, www.nytimes.com/2015/01/11/fashion/no-37-big-wedding-or-small .html?_r=1.

2. Tony Robbins, "Tony Robbins book excerpt: Questions are the Answer," *Fortune,* October 30, 2014, http://fortune.com/2014/10/30/tony-robbins-money-master -the-gme/.

3. John C. Maxwell, *Good Leaders Ask Great Questions* (New York: Center Street, 2014), 7.

4. Michael Bosworth and Ben Zoldan, *What Great Salespeople Do: The Science of Selling Through Emotional Connection and the Power of Story* (New York: McGraw-Hill Education, 2012), 142.

5. Mark Gibson, "Why Salespeople Fail—Failure to Listen to Premature Elaboration—Mike Bosworth Webinar," *Advanced Marketing Concepts*, June 3, 2013, www.admarco.net/resources/company-news/bid/97474/Why-Salespeople -Fail-Failure-to-Listen-Premature-Elaboration-Mike-Bosworth-Webinar.

6. Arman Sadeghi, "6 Rules of Pain and Pleasure—The Science Behind All Human Action," *Titanium*, December 5, 2015, https://titaniumsuccess.com/6-rules-of -pain-and-pleasure-the-science-behind-all-human-action/.

Chapter 8: Emotional Commitment Creates Urgency

1. John Sherill, "Bruce Renfroe," *Guideposts*, January 2001: 61–64, www.hudsons class.com/Documents/Freshman/Renfroe.pdf.

2. "The Science of Listening," *Korn Ferry Institute*, November 8, 2012, www.korn ferry.com/institute/514-the-science-of-listening.

3. Paul J. Zak, "How Stories Change the Brain," *Greater Good Science Center*, December 17, 2013, http://greatergood.berkeley.edu/article/item/how_stories _change_brain.

4. Shari Levitin, "The 5 Secrets of an Effective Sales Story," *Shari Levitin*, www .sharilevitin.com/blog-news/sales-management-training/effective-sales-story/.

5. Interview with author. Used with permission.

Chapter 9: Changing the Terms Requires a Change in Emotional State

1. Pamela Meyer, "How to spot a liar," TED video, 18:50, filmed July 2011, posted October 11, 2011, www.ted.com/talks/pamela_meyer_how_to_spot_a _liar?language=en.

2. Mike Weinberg, *New Sales. Simplified.: The Essential Handbook for Prospecting and New Business Development* (New York: AMACOM, 2012), 154.

Chapter 10: Looking for Wrongs Never Makes You Right

1. Steven Pressfield, *The War of Art* (New York: Black Irish Entertainment LLC, 2011).

2. Dan Baker, *What Happy People Know: How the Science of Happiness Can Change Your Life for the Better* (New York: St. Martin's Griffin, 2004), 100.

3. Brad Stone and Sarah Frier, "Facebook Turns 10: The Mark Zuckerberg Interview," *Bloomberg Businessweek*, January 30, 2014, www.bloomberg.com /news/articles/2014-01-30/facebook-turns-10-the-mark-zuckerberg-interview.

4. Katherine Harmon, "How Important Is Physical Contact with Your Infant?" *Scientific American*, May 6, 2010, www.scientificamerican.com/article /infant-touch/.

5. Ira Glass, "513: 129 Cars," podcast audio, *This American Life*, MP3, 1:14:11, December 13, 2013, www.thisamericanlife.org/radio-archives/episode/513/129-cars.
6. David McRaney, "Confirmation Bias," *You Are Not So Smart*, June 23, 2010, https://youarenotsosmart.com/2010/06/23/confirmation-bias/.
7. Viktor E. Frankl, *Man's Search for Meaning* (Boston: Beacon Press, 2006).
8. Jonathan O'Connell, "When the titan wants to build the town: Under Armour founder Kevin Plank's $5.5 billion plan for Baltimore," *Washington Post*, July 29, 2016, www.washingtonpost.com/news/digger/wp/2016/07/29/when-the-titan-wants-to-build-the-town-under-armour-founder-kevin-planks-5-5-billion-plan-for-baltimore/.
9. David Brooks, *The Road to Character* (New York: Random House, 2015).

INDEX

Accountability, 34

Achievement, stress and, 211

Action, 145

Actionable value, 59-61

Adams, Lisa, 208

Adamson, Brent, 82

Add-ons, 140

Advantages, 174

Adventure, 55

Affection, 14-15

Agenda, 132

Aggression, 192

Agreement, gaining, 170

Allred, Ken, 125

Amygdala, 191, 197

Analysis paralysis, 190-191

Anchor, Sean, 210

Anger, 192

Apapacho, 14-15

Appreciation audit, 214, 215-216

Are You Really Listening?, 117

Assertion, 192

Attention span, 23-24

Attention, 26, 204-205

Authentic connection, 13

Authenticity, 16-17, 21, 65, 114

Baby negative, 140

Baker, Dan, 214

Balancing heart and sales, 13-15

Balancing rapport and urgency, 81-82

Beatles, the, 90

Beck, Martha, 141

Believing, 212, 213-214

Belonging, 49

Benefits, 174, 175, 188

Bias,

confirmation, 218

hindsight, 147

Big data, 63

Blame, 23, 33-36

Body language, 119, 170

Bosworth, Mike, 146

Brain, emotional, 51-53

Brain,
    human, 144
    triune theory of the, 75
Bridging statement, 199
Brooks, David, 222
Brynner, Yul, 99-100
Buying process, 74-75
Catron, Mandy Len, 143-144
Chailly, Ricardo, 41
Challenger Sale, The, 82
Challenging excuses, 192
Character, 225
Checklist Manifesto, 70-71
Checklists, 65, 66-68, 70-71
Chipotle Grill, 53
Choice, 20, 207, 225
Chronic laziness, 25
Closing, 184, 194
Cole, Sean, 218
Commitment to growth, 31-33
Commitment, 143, 176
    emotional, 163-182
    urgency and emotional, 19
Common ground, 116-117
Compassion, 21
Competency, 19, 105, 135-138
Concentration, 120, 191
Concerns, restating, 198-199
Concessions, 202
Confirmation bias, 218
Confirmation, information, 168-171
Confirming information, 80
Confusion, 187

Connection, 13, 56, 65, 66, 145
Connections, creating deeper, 213, 216-217
Consistency, 71
Constructive delusion, 213, 217-218
Constructive feedback, 44
Core motivators, 52-58
    mistakes and, 58-63
    price and, 61-62
Core objections, 184
Correctness, emotional, 107-108
Courage, 99-104
Creating deeper connections, 213, 216-217
Creativity, 101
Credibility, 134
Curiosity, 18, 29, 30, 31, 36-41
Curtain, Nan, 217
Customers, affection for, 14
Damasio, Antonio, 51
Decision-making, 150
    emotions and, 18, 49-64
Deeper connections, creating, 213, 216-217
Default mode network, 22
Default mode, 21-27
Delusion, constructive, 213, 217-218
Demonstrating value, 193
Desperation, 193-194
Dialogue, 118
DiMaggio, Joe, 100
Dimensions of listening, 118-120
Disconnection, 56

Discovery questions, 143, 147-148

Discovery, 80, 133, 147, 152, 166, 168-169, 173

Dixon, Mathew, 82

Dominant buying motive, 52, 121, 148, 156, 171, 173, 180

Donoghue, Paul, 117

Dropping the price, 183

Duhigg, Charles, 23

Dweck, Carol, 31

Education, 58

Effort, 188, 195

Ego, 22, 23, 42, 46-47

Eisler, Lee, 180

Embarrassment, 93
    state of, 190, 191

Emotional brain, 51-53

Emotional commitment, 163-182
    urgency and, 19

Emotional correctness, 107-108

Emotional Intelligence for Salespeople, 92

Emotional motivators, 52

Emotional state, change in, 20

Emotional states, negative buyer, 190-191

Emotional triggers, 122

Emotions, decision-making and, 18, 49-64

Empathetic emotional selling, 92

Empathy statement, 132

Empathy, 125
    trust and, 19, 105-123

Engagement, 145

Epictetus, 115

Ethics, 13, 17

Eulogy virtues, 222

Excuses, 100-102, 189
    challenging, 192

Expectations, 133
    realistic, 130

Failure, 32, 87

Fear of rejection, 99-104

Fear, 18, 62, 87, 91-93, 210, 221

Fear, state of, 190-191

Features, 174

Federal express, 128

Feedback loop, 167-168

Feedback, 44-45, 134

Ferry, Ken, 168

Fight-or-flight, 84, 92, 191, 211

Finding your purpose, 213, 220-223

First-level questions, 148, 149, 153, 155-156

Fixed mindset, 31-32

Focus, 191

Frankl, Viktor, 220

Franklin, Benjamin, 32

Freedom, structure and, 18, 65-85

Frustration, 93

Fulfillment, 209
    happiness vs., 222-223

Gaining agreement, 170

Gawande, Atul, 70

Go for No!, 95

Goals, stretch, 95

Goulston. Mark, 37

Gratitude, practicing, 212, 214-216

Greenberg, Herbert M., 23

Greitens, Eric, 34, 68

Growth equation, 29, 30-33

Growth mindset, 32

Growth, 58

      technique and, 18, 29-47

Habits, 22, 23

Happiness, 210-211, 225

      fulfillment vs., 222-223

      rituals for, 211-223

Hard sell, 108

Harrison, Sean, 78

Health, 56-57

Heart and sales, balancing, 13-15

Heart sell, 108

Heart work, 206

Helping brands, 126

Hidden objections, 148, 158

High-impact motivators, 52

Hill, Napoleon, 140

Hindsight bias, 147

Human brain, 144

Humiliation, 93

Humor, sense of, 101

Improvement, 29

Incentives, 203, 205

Indifference, 93

Information confirmation, 168-171

Information,

      confirming 80

      irrelevant, 58-59

      unimportant, 58-59

Insecurity, 62

Insights, 136

Integrity cleanse, 141

Integrity, 12-14, 19, 105, 138-141

Intent, 134-135

      statement of, 79, 131-134

Interest span, 24

Interest, 110

Interrupting, 118

Isolating techniques, 196-201

Jargon, 188

Jones, terry, 202

Judgment, 105, 110, 111, 112

Just Listen, 37

Knowledge, 58, 136

Knowledge, lack of, 22, 24-25

Kohn, Sally, 107

Konrath, Jill, 78

Korn Ferry Institute, 168

Labels, 111

Lack of knowledge, 22, 24-25

Laziness, 22, 25-26

Laziness, chronic, 25

Learning, 32, 39-41, 43, 58

Legacy, 222

Lehrer, Jonah, 38

Levitin, Dan, 26

Lies, 189-190

Liner, John, 87-88

Linking, 176, 179

Listening, 42, 63, 94-95, 97, 168, 198

      dimensions of, 118-120

      wholehearted, 105, 117-123

Loewenstein, George, 38

Logic, 51, 76, 77, 151

MacLean, Paul, 75

Man's Search for Meaning, 220

Manipulation, 13, 14, 198

Margenot, Maria, 73-74

Market share, 171-174

Mascia, Jason, 218

Master, 29, 30

Mastery, 18, 41-43

Maxwell, John, 145

Mayer, David, 23

McGriff, Joe, 84

McKee, Robert, 24, 118

Methodological questioning, 144

Meyer, Pamela, 189

Michelin, 54

Midbrain, 76-77

Mills, George, 106-107, 111

Mindset, 31

Mindset, 31-33

Mistakes, core motivators and, 58-63

Modifying terms, 183

Moonshot Factory, 103

Moral Molecule, 178

Motivation, 220, 152

Motivators, core, 52-58

Motivators, secondary, 62-63

Mr. Holland's Opus, 57

Multitasking, 26

Need, 186-187

Negative buyer emotional states, 190-191

Negotiation, 95

Nelson, Shasta, 216

Neocortex, 76-77

Neuroscience, 209-210

    curiosity and, 38

New Sales Simplified, 202

Nodding, 170

No-need objections, 186-187

Non-negotiables, 73-74

Nonverbal cues, 119, 171

Obama, Barack, 59

Objections, 88, 93, 96, 98, 140, 148, 158, 170

Objections,

    core, 184

    real, 195-201

One-upmanship, 112-112

Optimism, 209-210, 212

Paying attention, 26

Peak state, 78

Perspective, 184

    shift in, 15

Petress, Ken, 117

Phrasing, 176

Pires, Maria João, 41-42

Pivoting, 42

Plank, Kevin, 221

Point of reference, 174

Positivity, 209-210, 212

Possibilities, 145

Power of Habit, The, 23

Practicing gratitude, 212, 214-216

Premature Elaboration, 146

Pressfield, Steven, 210, 211

Pressure, 132, 133

Price,

    core motivators and, 61-62

    dropping the, 183

Primary Intelligence, 125-126, 135

Priorities, 154

Problems, solving, 213, 219-220

Process, 66-77

Productivity, 209

Promises, the right kind of, 129-130

Proposals, 203-204

Prospecting, 78-79, 96

Psychology, 69

Purpose, a sense of, 53, 57

Purpose, finding your, 213, 220-223

Questions, 143-162

    discovery, 19, 143, 147-148

Rackham, Neil, 146

Radiohead, 109-110

Rapport and urgency, balancing,
    81-82

Rapport, 108-116, 123, 143

Rational mind, 51

Rationality, 76, 77

Real objections, 195-201

Realistic expectations, 130

Rebuttals, 194

Receiving feedback, 44

Rejection, 221

    fear of, 99-104

Relationships, 56

Relevance, 181

Reliability, 19, 105, 127-131

Removing sales resistance, 202-205

Renfroe, Bruce, 163-165

Reptilian brain, 75-77

Requesting feedback, 134

Resilience, 34, 68

Resilience, 87, 145, 183, 184, 210

Resistance, removing sales, 202-205

Responsibility, 18, 23, 29, 30, 33-36

Responsiveness, 128-129

Restating concerns, 198-199

Resting state, 22

Resume virtues, 222

Right questions, the, 145

Rituals for happiness, 211-223

Rituals, optimism and, 211-223

Road to Character, The, 222

Robbins, Tony, 55, 144

Robertson, Adam, 193

Rowling, J.K., 89

Safety, 54

Said, the, 118, 119

Sales resistance, removing, 202-205

Sales, balancing heart and, 13-15

Samuelson, Paul, 141

Scarcity, 163

Science, 184

Scripts, 70

Secondary motivators, 62-63

Second-level questions, 148, 149, 155

Self-disclosure, 144

Selling, emotional, 92

Seninger, Glenn, 71

Sense of humor, 101

Sense of purpose, 53, 57

Shame, 93

Shift in perspective, 15

Siegel, Mary, 117

Significance, 53, 55

Skill, 225

Skinny branches, 87, 89

Smith, Frederick, 129

Social media, 216-217

Socrates, 144

Solving problems, 213, 219-220

Spin Selling, 146

Stanley, Colleen, 92-93

Statement of intent, 79, 131-134

Status quo, 126, 135, 187

Stories, 177-182

Story vault, 180

Stress, achievement and, 211

Stretch goals, 95

Strident Development Group, 145-146

Structure, freedom and, 18, 65-85

Success, 57, 210

Suspicion, state of, 190, 192

Takeaways, 140

Technical prowess, 74

Technique, growth and, 18, 29-47

Teller, Astro, 103

Tenacity, 101

Tendencies, 21-27

Tension, 131

Terms, modifying, 183

Think and Grow Rich, 140

Third-Level motivators, 52

Third-Level questions, 149, 153-156

Third-Level selling, 149-159

This American Life, 218

Triune theory of the brain, 75

Trust, empathy and, 19, 105-123

Truth, 179-180

Truths, universal, 15-20

Unconscious mastery, 42

Understanding, 117-118

Universal truths, 15-20

Unsaid, the, 118, 119-120

Unsayable, the, 118, 120

Urgency, 163-182

  balancing rapport and, 81-82

Urgency, emotional commitment

  and, 19

Value,

  actionable, 59-61

  demonstrating, 193

Values, 113-114

Virtues, 222

Waltz, Andrea, 95-96

War of Art, The, 210

Warm-up, 79, 109, 131, 166

Weinberg, Mike, 202

Wellness, 56-57

What Happy People Know, 214

White, Eric, 40

Wholehearted listening, 105, 117-123

WIFM, 53, 148, 166, 176

Winfrey, Oprah, 55-56

Xerox, 146

Zak, Paul, 178

Ziglar, Zig, 25

Zuckerberg, Mark, 215

Shari Speaks

Shari Levitin speaks frequently at sales conferences, sales kick-offs, and annual sales events. An acclaimed keynote speaker and motivator, Shari can customize her message to meet the needs of your sales reps or managers.

Shari will win over your team with her warmth, humor, and expert practical advice. Her highly interactive programs will ignite your team and teach them how to balance heart and authenticity with the need to roll up their sleeves and meet quota.

Management and Leadership

Exclusively for your management and leadership teams, Levitin Group will develop customized Train the Trainer webinars based on the Universal Truths. Boost excitement, and performance, by having the Levitin team perform live their two outstanding management workshops:

- "Showtime," will teach your leaders the four pillars of an effective training, coaching, and mentoring program. With more than 500 graduates world-wide, Showtime is hailed as the most comprehensive results-producing training program for trainers. *www.sharilevitin.com/live-training-products/*
- "Your Authentic Voice" Performed with TED coach Lee Eisler and Shari Levitin. This workshop addresses the need to present to customers with a shorter attention span than ever before. You'll engage in short lectures and discussions, along with skill-building exercises, combined with lots of opportunities for speaking using short impromptu studies and formal presentations.

Virtual Learning

If you're looking to create a culture of ongoing learning and development, harness Levitin Learning—a robust, virtual training platform that combines engaging video lessons with testing, monitoring, and reporting. Levitin Learning is filled to the brim with bite size learning modules that reinforce rapport building skills, Third Level questioning techniques, isolation methods to overcome objections, and ongoing motivation for your team. *www.sharilevitin.com/virtual-training/*

Open your heart and close more deals!

Free Resources

Visit ShariLevitin.com and download one or all of the following:
- The Show Must Go On eBook
- 7 Keys to beating Rejection eBook
- Third Level Selling: 25 Sales Questions Guaranteed To Unlock Your Customer's Needs eBook
- Ride Evaluation Form
- Top 35 Tendencies That are Costing You Sales

For more information on Shari and her programs go to *www.sharilevitin.com* or call 435-649-0003.